transient senses

an inquiry into
the emergence
of sense in/with
the barcelona pavilion
of mies van der rohe

alex arteaga

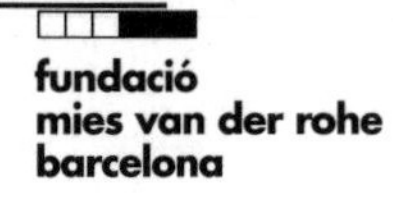

RM

table
of contents

introduction

This book is neither a catalog nor a documentation of *transient senses*, a research project in, with, and, in a certain sense, about the Barcelona Pavilion.[1] Instead, it is conceived as perhaps the last phase and last product of a process of inquiry that gave rise to this project, and that configures it. Like the other artifacts that inform *transient senses*—a sound installation, a text essay, a sound essay, and a video essay—this book is not understood as a container of knowledge, as is usually the case for the tangible outcomes of research projects. Knowledge can neither be produced nor contained. Knowledge is not an object, "such that [we] have in [our] possession the law of its making."[2] On the contrary, it emerges collectively out of our shared interaction with artifacts, as a new significance of what we consider to be the object of our inquiries. Knowledge is never "knowledge about" but a reconfiguration, a transformation, a relocation of what is intended to be known.

The book, like the other productions that articulate *transient senses*, is an element of contingency, a cognitive agent in an attempt to understand how interiority and exteriority arise in touch with the Barcelona Pavilion. As part of a field of shared agency, this book facilitates and requires the complicity of other agents—in this case, the community of readers—in order to co-constitute new significances of these terms and their processes of emergence, to open up these concepts, to make them available for reinterpretation and, on this basis, to establish new coherences within their (our) semantic field. This book aims to "talk with," to be a "con-dition," to interpellate the reader rather than to "be read" as an act of decoding. It intends to in-form, to be an active part of the process of in-formation instead of a collection of passive surfaces for the transmission of something made in advance, something closed, finished, and ready to be handed out.

1   The building designed by Mies van der Rohe as the German national pavilion for the 1929 Barcelona International Exhibition and reconstructed from 1983 to 1986.

2   Maurice Merleau-Ponty, *Phenomenology of Perception*, London and New York 1962, p. xi-xii.

The choice of the presence of interiority and exteriority in/with these specific constructed surroundings as the object of research of *transient senses* was made in the Pavilion. I did not choose this issue in advance and then look for a building to study it. On the contrary: I experienced the Pavilion in an unmediated and consistent manner and realized that the way in which the phenomena of interiority and exteriority emerge and relate to one another in interaction with this specific construction is its most relevant, unique, and intriguing trait.

Nevertheless, this choice was conditioned by the framework in which I made it: *Architecture of Embodiment*.[3] This is a research project—or, as I prefer to name it, a research environment configured by autonomous but interconnected single projects like *transient senses*—in which I approach architecture from an enactivist perspective. In its first three years of development (2013-2016), the focus was on the most basic constructive aspects of architecture: materiality, structure, form, and volume.

Enactivism, or more properly the enactive approach to cognition, is a conceptual framework according to which selves and worlds are understood as entities arising simultaneously through mutual specification. Selves and their worlds, worlds and their selves, are the emergent results of the dynamic coupling between autonomous systems—living beings—and heteronomous items—the components of their surroundings. Selves and worlds co-emerge. They are constituted in mutual determination, and this system-immanent process is understood as the process of cognition, or in other words, as the process of sense-making, which I prefer to denominate, stressing its inner structure, as the emergence of sense.

Departing from these ideas, which I have laid out here in a very succinct and simplified way,[4] the main question of *Architecture of Embodiment* is: How does architecture condition the emergence of sense? Or,

3   www.architecture-embodiment.org

4   For a fundamental and exhaustive account of enactivism, see Evan Thompson, *Mind in Life. Biology, Phenomenology and the Sciences of Mind*, Cambridge MA 2007.

how do constructed surroundings act as a constraint in the ongoing process of co-emergence of selves and worlds—of constitution of subjects and their environments? In contrast to other phenomenologically oriented inquiries on architecture, the main focus of *Architecture of Embodiment* is not architecture itself—posing questions such as how do we perceive architecture, or what does architecture mean for us— but the whole dynamic system of embodiment, constrained through the constructive alteration of the surroundings.

In this context, the research performed in/with the Pavilion can be considered as a case study. To research the way in which two concrete and basic phenomena like interiority and exteriority come to be in interaction with specific constructed surroundings allowed me to understand the process of formation of two concepts through the bodily experience of organized, large matter. In doing so, I retraced the process of the arising of meaning, or to be more precise, the constitution of its nuclear elements—concepts—back to its roots in the coupling between bodies and their surroundings. I started with the constituted phenomenon— with "the thing itself" ("die Sache selbst")—in order to inquire into its process of constitution. I started with the conceptual and the perceptual to access the operative. I moved from meaning to sense.

My research was facilitated by the crisis of the concepts of interiority and exteriority compelled by the Pavilion: the vagueness, ambiguity, and instability in which they arise in interaction with this construction. In, but much more with, this building, these phenomena do not appear as clearly contoured presences as is commonly the case. Interacting with other constructions, we do not doubt if we are inside or outside. But here these phenomena appear in an open, ambivalent way, not fully constituted, or better, constantly on the edge of their constitution. This unsteady state of the (quasi-)phenomena—their continuous circulation between not-yet-phenomena and no-longer-phenomena—provides unmediated accessibility to their processes of constitution—of differentiation, of objectification. The Pavilion helps to present these phenomena in their states of becoming, thus allowing for a first-person, sense-based inquiry into the agency of construction as an enabling condition for their emergence. In other words, the Pavilion facilitates aesthetic research on the function of the constructive alteration of the body's surroundings in the emergence of a subject and its environment—an aesthetic investigation of the emergence of sense in architectural context.

The Pavilion, thus, fulfills a twofold function in this research. On the one hand—as construction—it constrains, in a very particular way, the body that inhabits it and the body's relationship with its surroundings beyond the constructed field. On the other hand—as this specific organization of constructed matter—it configures an instrument of thought, a cognitive apparatus to reflect on its own agency as construction and, furthermore, on the general agency of construction in the process of the emergence of sense.

In *transient senses*, the Pavilion is understood and treated as the basic aesthetic dispositive, to which another dispositive—*transient senses*—is added in order to reinforce and extend its immanent cognitive agency. The artifacts that I produced—including this book—try to adapt to the Pavilion in the same way that new lenses adjust to an already configured microscope. In order not so much to see something different, but rather to increase the possibilities of what is seeing. This building is an exceptional construction that not only fulfills basic architectural functions and the representative purposes for which it was commissioned. Furthermore, it constitutes an apparatus to reflect (on) architecture. It is architecture thinking architecture. *transient senses* is an attempt to extend this cognitive potentialities with other means, that is, in other media—sound, video, written and dialogic language—activated through other practices—recording, editing, composing, installing, writing, conversing, dialoging, and debating.

Therefore, *transient senses* is exemplary of a certain concept of *artistic research,* or what I prefer to denominate as aesthetic research. I opt for this alternative formulation in order on the one hand to avoid the normativity implicit in the term "artistic" and thus the implicit inclusion of this kind of research in art's system, and on the other hand to stress the function of "aesthetics"—the sensorimotor activity of a body coupled with its surroundings in an unmediated and constitutive manner—as the roots of the research process. Nevertheless, the methodology developed for this project can be considered as hybrid. It results from the coexistence of aesthetic practices and practices originating in the humanities, especially phenomenology, enactivism, and philosophical aesthetics. The denomination "aesthetic" is justified precisely by the primacy of aesthetic practices in the process of inquiry, that is, their fundamental function in the research methodology. This manifests firstly in the performance of aesthetic research processes as the starting point of the inquiry, and therefore the constitution through this kind of practices of the materials and artifacts that operate as foundations for further research phases. Secondly, the preeminence of aesthetics is substantiated through the elaboration of what can be considered to be the "results" or "final conclusions" of the research process in interaction with the aesthetics artifacts that have been produced as constitutive elements of this process. These artifacts are treated here as cognitive agents of an open-ended process of the emergence of knowledge.

The choice of aesthetic practices as the main means of research in this project was, again, not made in advance. It results from the attempt to investigate the selected subject matter in a non-reductive way. Sense—this is my thesis—arises in an aesthetic cognitive sphere, or in other words, out of the most fundamental connective dynamics between body and surroundings. It is not present in a perceptual way or as the result of any other kind of objectifying intentionality, as meaning is, but operationally—implicitly, intrinsically integrated in the sensorimotor performance of the body to whom it appears, in its dynamic coupling with its emerging environment. Consequently, only through research practices performed on the same cognitive area, that is, activating the immanent epistemic potentialities of aesthetic action, is it possible to access sense as sense. The research of aesthetics must be based on aesthetic research.

Initially, before the publication of this book, *transient senses* was configured through four aesthetic artifacts and a research seminar. All these components are presented in this volume in different ways. The four productions—a sound installation, a text essay, a sound essay, and a video essay—were conceived, produced, and exhibited simultaneously, establishing a synergetic relation to one another and with the Pavilion. The research seminar took place during the public display of these productions, and was intensely related to them.

The **sound installation** in the Pavilion was configured by four pairs of microphones, each added to one of the "external" surfaces of its four glass walls and oriented in both longitudinal and cross-sectional directions. The microphones were connected one-to-one to four omniwave loudspeakers that, due to their specific construction and position, were able to create a fairly homogeneous sound field in the part of the building that can be considered its "interior." Additionally, the microphones were connected with a subwoofer in order to reproduce the lowest frequencies. Before the signals produced by the microphones arrived at the loudspeakers, they were processed by an algorithm written by Thomas Koch specifically for this project. Dynamically, meaning changing its range of effect in time, this algorithm modulated the sounds transmitted through the microphones in four different ways: reinforcing their interiority, that is the conditions for their perception as sounds heard in an interior space; intensifying their exteriority, that is the possibilities of their presence as sounds perceived in the open field; changing the connections between microphones and loudspeakers simultaneously in both dimensions—back to front and left to right; and, interrupting the sound reproduction completely from time to time, thus making it possible to hear (in) the Pavilion without the interference of the installation.

The function of this artifact—an intervention rather than an installation—was to reinforce aurally the instability of the presence of interiority and exteriority co-constituted by the Pavilion. It did not "add" anything to the Pavilion. It tried to "operate," to condition experience in the same way the Pavilion does, therefore enhancing its efficacy as cognitive apparatus. The radical site-specific nature of this intervention hinders its adequate presentation in another medium. Besides this short description, the installation is only presented in this book as photographs.

The **three essays**—sound, video, and text—described below were displayed in one space of the Fundació Antoni Tàpies. They were set up in a way that made it impossible to interact with two of them simultaneously as well as to induce movement from one to the others. I use the term "essay" here in its most basic and original meaning: to intend, to attempt, to try—"essayer"—to understand a specific issue without previously determined formal constraints and without aiming to achieve absolute conclusions. Accordingly, each essay is an autonomous, but intimately connected with the other components of *transient senses,* medium-specific and open-ended effort to create enabling constraints for the aesthetic investigation of their common subject matter.

The **sound essay** was composed by sequencing parts of sound recordings realized statically on different spots of the Pavilion during the night, between 2 and 5 a.m. In this time interval, the presence of singular, clearly defined sounds is reduced to a minimum, allowing focus on aural attention rather than auditory-spatial qualities. When "nothing sounds," or better when "no-things" sound, it is easier to hear the qualities of what "is sounding."
I chose the recording spots according to the different balance of interiority and exteriority of the aural presences they allow to appear. Accordingly, in this essay there is "no-thing" to hear. Instead, it provides conditions for a concentrated aural experience of the subtle behavior of inwardness and outwardness enabled by the Pavilion.

The **video essay** addresses the subject matter of this project through a similar compositional strategy—a sequence of static recordings. Each one faces either a constructively established limit of, and in, the Pavilion, or an interstice between two of these limiting elements. Like the sound essay, the video essay does not aim to "show anything." It mobilizes one of the most basic and inalienable procedures of the photographic and cinematic media—framing—to question the the blocking and enabling functions of these constructive elements and their apparently steady character. It creates a framework within which to observe their interlaced agencies—their contributions to the constitution of this place. The sound and the video essay are accessible through the links printed in the corresponding section of this book. They are stored in the Research Catalog of the Journal for Artistic Research.[5]

The **first text essay**, printed in this book with the original layout and pagination of its exhibition with the other two essays, is a the physical result of a process of aesthetically thinking the subject matter of *transient senses* through a practice of writing. It is the tangible product of a process of aesthetic inquiry performed in the medium of written language. It is an attempt to activate the resources of this medium—the conditions of possibilities it provides—in order to understand how the constructive components of the Pavilion—their dimensions, materiality, and organization—in interaction with my body—with the performance of its sensorimotor capabilities—make possible the appearance of these particular presences of interiority and exteriority. It is a way to deepen my memories, to revisit them, to re-member through the articulation of linguistic sings. An attempt to look into the embodied experience of inwardness and outwardness in order to trace back their processes of constitution by observing the arising configurations of words.

The practice of writing that generated this essay was a way to get in touch again with this organized matter, to reenact the contact with these architectonic elements and with the presences that this touch, this contact, this communication enabled to emerge. The text, the series of marked surfaces of contingency, aims to provide new material conditions for further reenactments, for getting-in-touch-at-distance(-again).

5   www.researchcatalogue.net and www.jar-online.net

The **second text essay** has been written for this book, starting from where the first ends. It was developed on the basis of the first, trying to extend its range of observation to the general field of architectural construction. Here, the attempt has been to perform the same kind of aesthetic writing but this time on an abstract level, taking abstractions as concrete matter of touch. This second essay is an effort to bridge *transient senses* and *Architecture of Embodiment*, to close the circle between both, addressing the questions of the second in the framework built by the first, observing-through-writing the insights it enabled. The process of writing this essay has been an attempt to reactivate the cognitive agency of the whole dispositive [Pavilion-*transient senses*] in order to understand how architecture conditions the emergence of sense, a new effort to thinking construction through the enhanced thinking of this thinking construction.

Both essays do not aim to "explain anything." They are another attempt to provide constraints for intimate observation—conditions for aesthetic conduct. Although the essays are developed in the medium of written language, they do not try to configure meaning, or at least not in a direct way. They intend to destabilize consolidated meaning as a condition of possibility for its new constitution.

The **research seminar** was divided into two parts. The first took place at the Barcelona Pavilion, the Goethe Institute in Barcelona, and the Fundació Antoni Tàpies, with the participation of Susanne Hauser, Dieter Mersch, and Gerard Vilar as experts. In interaction with the Pavilion, the sound installation, the essays, and the rest of the participants, we discussed on basic issues addressed in *transient senses* on the levels of both content and research methodology.

The second part took place in the Pavilion and the Fundació Antoni Tàpies as well, but also in the venue of Sónar+D—the international conference organized by the festival Sónar. Thanks to the expertise of Rudolf Bernet, Jean-Paul Thibaud, and Xavier Bassas, and the performative intervention of the sound artist Lucio Capece in the Pavilion, this section was especially devoted to the auditory aspects of *transient senses* approached from a phenomenological perspective. The whole research seminar, moderated by the project's curator Lluís Nacenta, configured a framework for language-based, discursive reflection that extended and complemented the fundamental aesthetic research. A video documentary realized by Adrià Sunyol and accessible, like the video and sound essays, through the link included in the corresponding chapter of this publication, presents not only the content of the dialogs but also the situations in which they developed.

The **photographs** that conclude this book were produced by Thomas Vilhelm. He observed the processes of realization of the sound installation and the sound and video essays, from their beginning with the first recordings and tests until their end with their public presentation. The selection and layout of the photographs printed in this book has been led by the same intention that guided the making of the artifacts they refer to: not so much to show what they were like and how they have been exhibited but rather to provide another kind of access to the research process they configured. This, therefore, is the main reason to have opted for a reduced number of images, and for a large format in proportion to the size of these pages: to create another space of reflective observation rather than, again, "showing some-things."

Alex Arteaga, August 2016

text essays

text essays

one

I walk through this place. I walk slowly, changing my direction frequently but softly. I rarely trace a straight line.
I walk in a fragmented rhythm. Fragmented but smooth. I often change my pace, but just minimally. I take some steps, slightly modify my direction, take some more steps—perhaps a little bit faster now—I slow down and stop, briefly. I walk again, stop again, this time for longer.

The direction of my steps is not determined by the establishment of clear aims, by the will to arrive at a certain spot. I do not walk towards anything. Or maybe I do, but neither following a previously made decision nor in order to be there, but, I guess, attracted or rather motivated by something. Something vague, something I cannot formulate precisely, something that eludes the clarity of some-thing, of a manifestly contoured object I could point to and grasp. I am motivated—moved—by the dynamic network of relationships I am in here, by the meshwork of relationships I become part of in walking through this place.

Walking through this place I am not explicitly aware of the reasons why I modify the direction of my steps or, minimally, their speed. I do not know why I stop and then why I walk again. I do not need to know. I do not need an explanation, a linguistic artifact mediating between me walking through this place and the way I do it. There is no gap in between that needs to be filled with an explanation. There is no certainty that needs to be consolidated by a clarification. There is no need to transform the operative certainty that supports my steps and emerges from my steps—my steps-through-this-place—into another kind of certainty, an explicit one, the apodictic certainty of a linguistic formulation.

When I walk through this place there is no need to support the way I do it, stating explicitly the reasons why I do it this way. They—I could say, assuming their autonomous existence instead of considering them as a product of language-based cognitive practices—seem to be implicit in the walking itself. In my walking-through-this-place: a coherent dynamic conjoining me and the place I walk through, arising out of the confluence of this place and myself, developing itself through this emerging coalescence as one of its enabling conditions and, simultaneously, as one of its emerging outcomes.

I look around by walking. I walk in this place looking at it. I look at its constructive elements—its walls, its ceilings, its water surfaces, its floor. My gaze dwells for a while on these elements, examining their color, their texture, their materiality, but these are not significant moments. Or at least not immediately significant to my relationship to this place. These are moments in which I am not in this place, in which the presence of the process of constitution of this place is momentarily suspended. Perhaps these moments configure a kind of background, a kind of silent foundation for my being-in-this-place, but in their actuality these are moments outside of it, pauses in my walking through this place, in my being in this place, in my being-with-this-place.

Facing the constructive elements, I end up looking through them. Furthermore, observing their organization, trying to figure out how they relate to each other, going from one to another, walking between them, looking at their relative positions, at the relationships between their limits, I end up beyond the surfaces and volumes they delimit, beyond the spaces they delineate, without abandoning this place, without ceasing to be in this place, but on the contrary being in this place only under these conditions, being-with-this-place under these very conditions.

I am in this place, I realize this place and myself being in it. Or to be more precise: I am, or better I become-with-this-place when, looking at it, walking in it, I look and walk through it. Through expresses my way of being in this place. Through is the specific variety of in and at that this construction enables, the variety of being here—of walking here, of observing here—that allows me to be on this constructed piece of land being in a place—on this piece of land marked and conditioned by construction. Through is the manner of being here that allows me to be here being-with-this-place, or trying again to be more precise, becoming-(myself)-

with-this place. To walk-through, to look-through are the speci-
fications of my walking-in and my looking-at that emerge out
of my interaction with the organization of the constructive
elements I encounter here, transforming the here they mark, delimit, and articulate in this very place—in this place-becoming-
itself—transforming my walking and observing into practices
of becoming-(myself)-with-this-place. A place becoming itself-
for-me, for this my-self which is becoming itself, itself-with-
this-place-(becoming-itself).

I transit this place. This place constitutes itself through my transit—the transit of my walking body, the transit of my sight—
which in turn is enabled by the possibilities that the constructive
elements I encounter here and their organization provide.
Walking through this place, looking through this place, I transit
a flow of openings and closures. Stopping in certain spots I can
experience an absolute closure or a total openness. But I just stop
momentarily, as an inflection of my walking-through. When I
walk again, the provisory, fragile—I could even say illusory—stability of an absolute closure or a total openness vanishes after the
first steps. A small displacement of my body, or simply a slight
turn of my head, or even a minimal movement of my eyes suffices
to destabilize the unambiguousness, to introduce an element of
crisis in the absoluteness of a sense of being inside or being outside induced and supported by a momentary, but in its actuality
unquestioned, perception of closure or openness.

Say I am facing a wall delimited by two perpendicular ones or a corner configured by two opaque walls apparently sustaining an equally opaque ceiling—say I am facing an enclosed space—I see a clear separation between this space and the rest of the world. Say these perceptions are stable, so stable that they lead to considering the space I am facing—the space I am in—as a closed one. Say I now take a step back, or turn my head slightly, or minimally change my visual focus.

These small actions suffice to introduce a fissure into the closure. They provoke a rearrangement of the walls, a virtual displacement that connects the excluded outside world to the darker, apparently protected area I am—I was—in.

An incipient opening appears, softening the closure, expanding the field. Without eliminating the presence of the closure but just endowing it with the enriching quality of doubt, of the fragile, of the transitory.

I step back. I turn slightly and cross the space that appeared closed. I go through it with my sight without abandoning it completely.

Challenging the unquestioned presence of the closure, reestablishing its fluid relationship with the openness, I reengage the flow that generates this place, that allows me to be-(myself)-with-this-place, that allows us—this place and me—to continue relating to each other, to continue becoming with one another, to continue emerging together. In transit—in transits. Transitorily.

The transition from an absolute, static closure to an ambivalent, vibrating closure-openness can equally occur without any bodily movement, even without any displacement of my sight. A slight change of light produced by the progression of the sun or the passing of a cloud might bring a different part of the pavilion onto the surface I am facing, and introduce openings in the closure I am—I was—in. The garden or the small basin might appear in front of me. Then I could see, in the middle of this closure, the exterior light reflecting on the ivy leaves or a small section of the trees delimited by the ceiling and the wall—another wall, behind and now also in front of me, partially illuminated by the sun. I see the trees moved by the wind, merged with the profiles of the crystal wall their image has to cross in order to arrive at the now mirroring wall in front of me.

I do not cease to be where I was. I do not feel disoriented. I feel my feet stable on the same hard surface they were on before these new presences appeared, relativizing the interiority of the situation I am—I was—in. Again, without eliminating it but questioning its unambiguousness, its categorical—even ontological—clarity: "I am inside"; "this is an interior, closed space." Being in it I go through it again as a coherent way to be in it.

Opaqueness—polished, gleaming opaqueness—transparency, mirroring. Again terms denoting qualities usually appearing in reciprocal opposition that manifest here in a multidimensional fluent continuity. On the one hand coexisting in each view, complementing one another, succeeding each other while I walk through. On the other hand, and more fundamentally, coexisting in one surface, appearing on the same surface simultaneously and in succession.

I look at an opaque wall. I only see this wall. The light changes, and I begin to see something else that the wall begins to mirror. The reflected image on the opaque surface—still present as opaque, manifesting its own structure—presents another opaque surface, perhaps reflecting a third one, perhaps crossing another, transparent one. The light changes again, and the transparent surface now mirrors the one I am facing, hindering the appearance of the surface that could be seen through the one that is now reflecting and is, for me here, no longer transparent.

A flow of transformations that in-forms the place I am transiting as a transitory one and as a place of transit, of transits.

The fluctuation between opaqueness, transparency, and mirroring: another variety of action of the constructive elements I interact with here. Another form of conditioning my walking-through, my looking-through. Another form of actively constraining my conduct, conditioned in turn by the changing light surrounding this construction, enveloping it, touching it, piercing it, crossing it, relating our reciprocal transit—this place transits me as well. It goes—through my temporary perceptions and interpretations, through the places I inhabit while transiting this place—to other, also reciprocal transits: that of this place through the day and the transit of the quotidian through this place.

The questioning of the closure that transitorily characterizes the space delimited by these solid opaque walls and ceiling I am partially surrounded by can occur in a third manner. This third possibility implies, as its condition of possibility, a modification of the balance between sensory modalities. The primacy of the visual—I walk through this place looking through it—has to be substituted by the preeminence of the auditory. Without ceasing to look at the walls I am facing—or to stop feeling the moderate, slightly oscillating warmth and smelling the freshness of the garden (it is 10.15 a.m., spring, and it rained last night) mixed with the emissions of the cars, buses, and motorcycles circulating behind it—the focus of my attention unexpectedly changes to the auditory. Perhaps the abrupt appearance of a loud incisive barking of two dogs playing on the esplanade, or of the strident yelling sounds produced by an ambulance, or the percussive metallic sounds generated by the string of one of the big flags hitting the mast repeatedly, moved by the strong squally wind, spontaneously attracts my attention. Sounds coming from somewhere else that cross the space I am in, extending it, connecting it to other spaces, beyond the limits that configure the transitory isolation, the closeness of this space I am—I was—in, the space I begin now, again, to transit, following the invisible line that connects the sounds I hear with the objects that produce them.

But again the crisis of the closure does not mean its obliteration. It just creates a dynamic tension, a questioning, an oscillation, an ambiguousness.

The sounds I am hearing now are clearly not produced where I am. They do not necessarily belong to the space I am in. The space is now, at least partially, open. But the sounds I spontaneously recognize as being produced somewhere else and as usually produced in an open field—as being exterior sounds—do not sound exactly as I would hear them where they are generated. There is an in-betweenness in the sounds I hear. There is an in-betweenness in my perception of the space I am in—I go through, again—induced by the in-betweenness of the spatial quality of the sounds I am listening to.

It is not that I am simply listening to sounds from the outside inside. This is what would happen if I were in my living room, for example. There, the solidity of the closure, the categorical, unequivocal affirmation of the inwardness cannot be questioned by the undeniable outwardness of the sounds penetrating that space. Their presence is not able to question the categorical manner in which both sides of the closure—the inside and the outside—are perceived. Here, on the contrary, due to the immanent fragility of the closures arising out of my transit through the openings provided by the organization of the constructive elements of the place I am in—I become-with through my transit— the presence of these sounds, generated outside and conditioned by the constructive elements that configure these fragile closures, breaks the categorical absoluteness in which my perceptions of closure and openness—and further on inwardness and outwardness—usually appear.

My awareness during the transit through the space I am in of the sounds I am hearing now as being produced on the one hand beyond the elements that enclose this space, and as exterior sounds—sounds that are usually produced in open spaces—and on the other hand, but simultaneously, as sounds slightly colored by a closure—not only by the influence of a single wall but by the conjunction of at least two of them—and consequently as interior sounds—sounds heard in an enclosed space—destabilizes the presence of the space I am in as an enclosed one, as an interior. This delicately enclosed space acquires a transitory, unstable character once again. The steadiness of its closure, of its inwardness, established spontaneously when I stopped here—when my stopping here and the organization of these walls and ceiling related to one another in such a way that enabled the emergence of this closure—is now questioned by the sounds I am hearing, or to be more accurate, by the precise way I hear these sounds, by the very specific quality and significance they acquire in this very specific context.

My listening, activated and modulated by the activity of entities beyond these walls, brings me back on the way that bought me here. It reactivates my transit through this place, my transit through its openings and closures, presenting again the transient nature of the transitorily constituted closure I am—I was—in. The one I am transiting now, again.

And on the other side of the walls I was facing, which are now, after taking a few steps, on my right, there is a new presence, a shadow, moving slowly, slower as I do, echoing my own displacement, marking resolutely but transitorily a new border, a new ambivalent sign—connecting as well as dividing, being there, on this surface, but presenting another one. A shadow reinforcing the opaqueness of the surface it touches, enabled by the same relationship between light and another opaque surface that, on its other side—I saw it few seconds ago—reflects the light falling on another surface, illuminated by the same light that is occluded here to form this shadow. The same light, the same surface, subtly creating here an even more fragile closure surrounded by openness and, on the other side, bringing openness into a tenuously enclosed area.

With the same smoothly fractioned rhythm in which I walk through this place, this place constitutes itself through my walking-through and through its transit through the day—and through the days—as a succession of intimately intertwined, ambivalent and vibrating closures and openings, heres and theres, closenesses and distances. Both—this place and I—transit a series of subtle, transitory, and interleaved stages defined by a lack of categorical definition, by a vibrating balance between perceptions that in another environment would appear as reciprocally excluding, as incompatible presences, but that coexist here in a constant flow of mutual penetrations. We both—this place and I, this co-emergent I-becoming-myself-with/through-this-place-becoming-itself—are constantly in a dynamic in-between, transiting a continuous variation of balances between apparently opposite perceptions that does not appear here as such but as elements of contingency in the emergence of this place, in my transit through this place, in my emergence-with-this-place.

The walls I encounter—mainly them, but also the ceiling they apparently support, and also the basins—are factors of contingency, elements of intimate touch that condition my walking, my looking, my listening. They provide the possibility of beginning to walk, to look, and to listen through rather than in(to), out, at, to(wards), or even across or around. My walking-through, my looking-through, and my listening-through, in turn, activating with their own development the potentiality generated by the materiality and organization of the constructive elements, reinforce their contingent character and minimize the possibilities of actualizing their containing potential. They minimize it but they do not block it; they do not obliterate it. They allow their contingent potentiality to prevail without eliminating their containing capability.

The materiality and disposition of these constructive elements condition my transit—its direction, its rhythm—fostering the maintenance of its own dynamic, subtly encouraging me to continue moving through this place rather than enclosing me in or excluding me from containing spaces, rather than situating me in clear insides or outsides.

The reciprocal touch, the mutual contingency established between my activity and the activity of these walls creates the conditions of possibility for a very specific variety of relationship between usually antipodal perceptions: compression and expansion, protection and exposure, distance and closeness, openness and closure, here and there, here and not-here. In this place they appear neither as stable nor as mutually excluding perceptions. They appear with the same contingent quality that characterizes the enabling conditions of their emergence—the constructive elements of this place and my transit through it.

The parallel walls on the longitudinal dimension—what I consider to be the foundation of the constructive structure of this place—due to their subtle displacement—with only one exception, the end points are out of alignment—and the alternation of their materials—glass, green marble, onyx, glass again (this time slightly colored), travertine, green marble again (but another kind)—do not appear in opposition to each other. Or to be more precise, they confront each other just enough to make a subtle tension possible, to generate a potential valence, a latent vector, a directional affordance that my transit operatively realizes as its own direction. I transit this place laying down ephemeral paths modulated by the surfaces and limits of the walls I encounter.

This relationship between the constructive elements and my transit already begins when I try to access this place. In this moment I face a platform elevated enough to appear as an obstacle but not sufficiently to be an insuperable one. Rather, it induces my movement to the right until I reach a first limit, and then to the left, where I find an opening structured by a few steps to access the platform. This is the initial moment in which a dynamic pattern, or better a framework of conduct is subtly induced. A framework of conduct that will develop itself in a virtuosic but discrete way on the platform, facing other surmountable obstacles—the walls—walking through the interstices they place at the disposal of my transit.

The transformation of the visual presence of the walls—their own transit through the states of opacity, transparency, and reflection originated by their transit through the day, by their interaction with the light—and the specific presence of the sounds in this place—endowed with a variable inwardness and outwardness—reinforce the dynamic I have just described. I face an opaque wall. I see the forms on the surface that its inner structure determines. But I simultaneously see another wall reflected on it. I turn and walk through the interstice both delimit, turn further on, and face the second one, the transparent one, and then I see children playing on the esplanade. I hear their voices, but slightly colored, with some common quality to the smooth voices I hear now behind me. I turn to them and see some people speaking between four walls: three are parallel but shifted, and the other one perpendicular, joining one of them. I see the wall I saw before—now it is not reflecting anymore— a second one partially illuminated, divided into different zones by light, a third one in twilight, and a fourth one, between them, at the back, simultaneously letting me see the garden through it and reflecting the other ones, the one behind me, and myself in between, somewhere in the in-betweenness configured by these ambivalent walls. A unique, dynamic in-betweenness I now begin to inhabit, transitorily.

Being here, perhaps moving minimally, slowly, slightly focusing my attention on the different surfaces I am facing, on the different spaces that disclose themselves on and through these surfaces around me, but without losing my awareness of the whole they configure, inhabiting this place—in-habiting it: letting this place modulate my embodied habits, letting myself realize them in this place, with this place—I am at the same time in another in-betweenness, in an in-betweenness arising from the one configured by the perceptual, dynamic coexistence of different spaces, from the different coexistent fragments of this place. It is an in-betweenness in a perceptual in-betweenness, intimately linked with it.

This other in-betweenness is enabled by my self-awareness in this specific situation, and is therefore constituted by the presence for myself of the very specific way I am here, by the presence of how it is to be-here-for-me. The presence of this complex dynamic system—I-with-this-place—appears now—and every time in which, being here, I achieve an awareness of the whole system, of myself-being-with-this-place—as fundamentally ambivalent and unstable. It appears as a dynamic network of coexistent qualities, which usually manifest excluding each other instead of, as they emerge here, complementing each other, being simultaneously present in an ever-changing balance, flowing into one another, blurring the limits of their categorical differences.

In this moment, this place, with which I am here, appears to be simultaneously compressing and expanding. I feel the muted pressure of the walls, the ceiling, and the floor, and at the same time the open space beyond them, the extension of this minimally compressed piece of world to the world beyond its fragile borders, the openness through these slightly containing elements. The presence of this place I am with now is both centrifugal and centripetal. It leads simultaneously to concentration, to focusing on a diffuse center—on blurry centers subtly constituted by the relationship between the constructive elements and my position now, surrounded by them—and to dissemination, to moving through these thin solid sheets, which partially enclose me, to their other side. It leads to constriction, confinement, and simultaneously to release. To intimacy, to privacy, and at the same time to participation in the collective dynamics surrounding the walls that are surrounding me now. More fundamentally, this place radically alters the relation between the centrifugal and the centripetal through a softening of its inner center, through the establishment of a balance between its almost neutralized attractive force and the agency of the exterior, and therefore through a minimization of the possible tension between center and periphery. It substitutes this tension through a gentle flow that never totally occludes one of the poles between which it oscillates, reducing to a necessary minimum their mutual distinction.

I walk through this place. I look through it by walking. I listen. I feel subtle changes of temperature when I cross the lines the sun traces touching the walls, the ceiling. I also feel the wind, even though I am close to the onyx wall—in this ambivalent inside—seeing through the transparent, lightly blue-colored glass wall how the trees' branches move—in this ambiguous exterior.

Transiting this place, letting this place emerge through my transit, letting my own emergence be modulated by the emergence of this place, I begin to relate in a different way to the concepts that articulate my thinking about the (built) environment.

They acquire another kind of presence. They begin to lose their stability, their clearness, their unambiguousness. Their contours, their definitional boundaries, begin to blur. Their limits begin to lose their containing function.

They do not vanish. They still allow me to refer to each concept as singular. They still contain their respective meaning, or at least what I could call their core meaning, their minimal meaning, their basic anchorage in the semantic field. But their boundaries begin to transform into elements of communication, into elements of touch rather than of separation, isolation, self-definition. Participating in the emergence of this constructed surroundings as a place, as an environment—as my environment—the membrane that contains each concept, that demarcates its particular field of significance becomes gradually permeable.

Concepts open up. Being here, becoming-with-this-place, the concepts that found and structured my thinking about place, site, environment, space, disclose themselves. They become available for redefinition, for the emergence of new concepts, and the establishment of new relationships between them. Without trying to rethink them. Without effort. Passively. Letting them evolve, adapt. To each other. To my being-with-this-place. Just being here in the way it is possible to be here (for me). Transiting. Walking through, looking through, listening through.

Concepts open up for new understandings. For a new positioning in the process of becoming-this-place-with-me. For a new way of conditioning our mutually determining transit. Opening new possibilities for our mutual adaptation that, in turn, enable new openings, new realignments, new configuration of their significances.

After a while, a silent while, some laconic expressions arise out of my transit through this place. I continue not needing any explanation about the reasons why I move here the way I do, about the specificity of my being-with-this-place.
These expressions are not explicatory. They connote rather than denote. They constitute new elements of touch, of subtle contact, rather than grasping or controlling. They do not arise with the purpose of fixing a meaning but rather with a purposiveness without purpose that enables the maintenance, even the intensification of a subtle presence: the implicit, operational awareness of myself transiting this place, of myself being transited by it. The tacit, subtle awareness of a stream of sense emerging amidst our co-emergence.

These linguistic expressions—constituted by virtue of the increasing ambivalence, of the expanding potential for redefinition of the concepts that inform them—configure a new dimension of the presence of my being-with-this-place, a new kind of awareness of my transit, of my con-duct—of the very specific way I lead myself with this place. And furthermore, a new kind of awareness of the viability of my conduct: of the possibility of a new step, of the plausibility of a new (in)sight.

Renewing, reshaping the presence for myself of my being-with-this-place, these expressions configure a new base, a viable trace for understanding inwardness and outwardness. For how they arise, relating to each other, as essential, constituting, emerging qualities of this place.

These expressions are not explanations, but they provide a new base—a foundation rooted in the immediate, bodily, intimate participation in the emergence of this place—for the formulation of alternative ones.

two

A body gets in touch with an alteration of its surroundings. An alteration produced by construction: a deliberate organization of material configurations bigger and harder than the body it encounters.
Or, described in a way that emphasizes continuity: the surroundings of a body are modulated through construction.
What this body encounters, what it is in touch with now, is not only planned, organized, ruled. It is not only structured. It is constructed.

This body encounters shaped matter. Compounded, configured material elements organized, related to one another by other bodies. Deliberately. Intentionally.

Large-sized material configurations. Exceeding the dimensions of the body. Occasionally only of some of them. But if we consider as a unit the totality of organized matter the body encounters now, it definitely exceeds the dimensions of the whole body.
Confronting it. Facing it. Offering resistance. Damming, occasionally letting pass—the whole body, the perturbations of its surroundings that can touch it, still, again, but now through constructed matter. Perhaps also receiving, including, enveloping, containing. Surrounding it completely. Establishing themselves as surroundings. Configuring new surroundings for the body. Inducing this body to be the body of these new surroundings. Substituting, transitorily—maybe only for an initial moment, maybe for much longer—the surroundings this body was in touch with by new ones. Constructed ones.

New surroundings, in turn, in touch with the ones the body just abandoned—temporarily, partially. The ones the body crossed to come here. Or better, again emphasizing continuity, the ones with which the body came here. Those with which the body has been becoming the body that now gets in touch with their constructive alteration. Those that, somehow, retreat now. At least for a moment. Those now, somehow, in crisis due to the new contacts, to the new encounters. Those which, after a while or perhaps immediately, will be redefined, resituated, eventually becoming surroundings of surroundings instead of unmediated surroundings of the body. Or maybe they will disappear, will be substituted, occluded; losing—at least in the meantime, at least apparently—any kind of factual agency in relation to this body.

Those that, as the body does, in any case acquire a position in relation to the new ones. Those that begin to be present in relation to the new ones and not only, as previously, to the body. Those that, perhaps—if the new ones enclose the body enough—will appear out there now, configuring a possible exteriority and thus co-creating the possibilities for a plausible interior, which in turn, initiating an endless, subtle feedback, will reinforce and maintain the presence of an exterior.

Those, in any case, surrounding—supporting, enveloping, confronting, compressing, expanding, crossing, piercing—no longer directly the body but also these specific, constructed ones—their constructive alteration, this more or less emancipated, autonomous variation that the body encounters now bringing both, consequently, into mutual relation.

The body, thus, is in touch with surroundings that are in touch with surroundings, which are in turn in touch with the body through the new ones.

The constructive alteration of the surroundings generates the possibility of new (kinds of) relationships, of new contingencies.

It intervenes in the coupling of body and surroundings, diversifying the possibilities of their interaction, offering new potential forms of touch, new ways in which the body can relate to what had been its surroundings to what, somehow, continues being its surroundings, but now in an altered, potentially expanded but in any case constrained way.

Construction as difference. As the introduction of a difference. As a way to differ—to set apart, to carry away, in another direction. To set asunder—to divide, to dissociate. Without breaking but rather deferring—delaying, postponing, shifting. Distancing. Or perhaps bringing closer, intensifying the previous connections. Diversifying. Offering new chrono-topological possibilities. Interstices. Potentialities of new forms of conjunction. Of new ways to refer to one another—body and surroundings. To trace back. To commit to one another— again. To (re) direct—again and again—to one another and beyond.

Construction as inter-ference. As a condition of possibilities of new ways to strike, to bore, to pierce each other—body and surroundings. And, in turn, out of this alteration: construction—struck, bored, pierced. Holed, punched, perforated, knocked, taped, marked, hit, pounded—from "both sides," or better: from the unstoppable dynamics of intimate contact between surroundings and their body.

Con-structed surroundings, structured-in-common by multiple actors on multiple levels: in the past—the past of the body that encounters them now—by those other bodies—the ones who conceived its particular organization, the ones who materialized it and their, somehow, common context; in the present, by the body that encounters them and by its former surroundings. Those that the body brings with itself as itself, as embodied surroundings, and that, simultaneously, through the topographic position the body takes now, due to the current actualization of its sensorimotor skills, the body puts in touch with the new, constructed ones, with their own constructive variation. A whole system of con-struction con-structing. Con-stituting—seeing up, placing, allowing to stand.

Construction con-straining, binding together the whole system and at the same time giving rise to new possible developments—of the whole system and of its parts. And simultaneously construction constrained by the system it now becomes part of—the ongoing dynamics of body and surroundings that flood the constructed now, re-con-structing it, providing new conditions for new constitution.

Construction, thus, con-ditioning and con-ditioned. Talking with each other—the body and the surroundings, both surroundings. Providing "arguments"—following the metaphor routed in the etymology—to one other in order to become, to change, to stay, to move. New possibilities for the dia-log, the transit-through-the-speech, across the spoken, through what is said and can be said in the middle—in medium—of the con-versation—the living in common, the shared life, the life supported now by this threefold.

Construction as condition of possibility of com-prehension, of grasping each other—of grasping and being grasped, by oneself, by others—through multiple possible modalities of touch, of multiple viable con-tacts. Of new possibilities of holding-together, of co-hering, of co-herence. Body, constructed surroundings, and the surroundings apparently, only topologically beyond but also here, also operatively present—touching each other, grasping each other. Oscillating between contingency and containment. Providing, by virtue of these complex oscillations, new crises and new temporary stabilizations of each component, of the whole system. Defining and destabilizing each other, articulating a never-ending dynamic system.

Construction, therefore, not only because of the assemblage of materials but also, now, in the actuality the body brings forth, because of the con-tact between multiple agents—the surroundings surrounding it, the body con-necting both, establishing both as its surroundings.

Interfering media: the body as medium—bringing surroundings in touch; the construction as medium—between the body and its former and future surroundings, its present-but-distant, present-but-mediated ones; and the surroundings of the construction as medium—between the construction and their common body, the body they share.

Three media not only for their respective in-betweenness but more fundamentally due to the potentialities they afford one another and the possible new relationships they might establish. Or better, re-inforcing continuity once again, overcoming the duality between relationships and the terms they connect, due to the new possibilities for their intrinsically relational respective ownnesses. And beyond, for the dynamic system they enable and that sustains them.

Three media configuring each other. Reciprocating their respective mediations, being media due to the mediation of what they mediate. Three fields of potentialities, of mutually constraining constraints. And also three possible perspectives of observation, three feasible, autonomous but—better and—fundamentally connected approaches to the system they configure and through which they are configured in their respective actualities.

Body, constructed surroundings and the surroundings beyond—the former and future surroundings, the surroundings underneath, the circumscribing surroundings—as reciprocating media and as such invisible, necessarily losing their respective entities in order to become media, the ownnesses whose development they mutually nourish in becoming media.
"I do not see the walls, I do not see myself, I do not see the trees." Of course I see them but they are no longer significant as single walls, as a single body, as single trees, and that is why "I do not see them." They rather turn out to be operative presences. Presences dynamically dependent on one another, bringing one another into presence or, to be more precise, bringing into presence the radically processual coher-ence that relates one to another, that holds all of them together, and by virtue of which they appear now—anew, re-newed, in a new manner. I can recognize the trees. I could say, "I have seen them before." But I do not say that. Probably I do not say anything now. Perhaps because the trees are no longer the same. Because somehow I too am no longer the same and neither are these walls. This is not a difference I can ob-jectify, at least not right away. It is, perhaps, a difference that does not

need to be objectified—to be grasped, to be con-ceptualized. It is more of a difference in my (our) operativity, in the manner we—my body, the walls, the trees—relate to each other. It is rather a relational change. Relational in a double sense: produced by relations and affecting these relations. And—once again reinforcing continuity—through these altered relations the related terms, which, after a while, when this alter-ation of the dynamics of coherence that bring and hold us together—the body, the walls, the trees—have sedimented, when the alteration has been stabilized, will bring forth new forms, new significances suitable for their constitution as transformed conceptual objects—new bodies, new walls, new trees—that I will "see" (again).

An agent of a cognitive apparatus. Construction—the preliminary of architecture, the "tekton," the texture, the woven, the made, the structured—as constraint of thought. As the introduction of a per-turbation in an ongoing process of shared constitution, of a dynamic, transformative coupling. A solid, silent and, by virtue of its solidity and silent standing, interpolating intervention in a closed, self-generated process. A free-standing, consistent element of potential disturbance with a double function. The first: to question the stable order, to alter an unquestioned steadiness—the sedimented arrangement between body and its surroundings, between surroundings and their body; to destabilize the established, introducing new possibilities of relation, extending the domain of communication.

The second: to actualize the potentialities facilitated by unlocking the habitualized, by destabilizing the sedimented. To allow new presences to arise, new possible bodies and surroundings to appear to the body as body, and beyond, as subject to which the body appears—as a part of itself, as a belonging, as a container, as a medium, as an instrument, as it-self—as its surroundings do as well—as an environment, as the world, as the abutting, immediate, actual world (as the "Umwelt," the world-around) of the subject.

Fragile, precarious but autonomously organized organic matter gets in touch with hard, solid, compacted, heteronomously organized matter. Moving, sensing matter encounters steady, firmly anchored matter. To refer to the first as "adaptable matter" would not be accurate enough. The differentiation between this kind of organized matter and its capabilities is a product of the medium in which this differentiation is established, generated—a certain kind of (written) language. This is also the case when the formulation is underpinned by a casual relationship based on the form of organization of the organic matter: "This matter is adaptable due to its form of organization." Nothing wrong with that.

Nevertheless, it is possible to approach this question differently, forcing the hard walls of syntax a little and writing something like "autonomously organized matter is adaptation." Adaptation to itself and to the other—accepting again a categorical differentiation that could equally be questioned. Organic matter is a process of adaptation, of extremely subtle, continuous, complex, multidimensional, and spontaneous tuning.

Accepting the constraints of the linguistic medium, it is possible to situate adaptation in the "base," at the bottom of the formulation instead of placing it at the top.

Going a step further, inevitably accepting the constraints of the medium in which this is going to be manifest now, the following formulation is possible: "organic matter is embodiment"—the embodiment of its own process of adaptation. Formulating it now as a circle, as an attempt to escape the inexorable linearity of the medium: "organic matter embodies the process of adaptation that it enables and that enables it—its embodiment." And in doing so it embodies the objects of adaptation: itself and its surrounding—what touches it, what is around it and reaches it, what actively circumscribes it.

A complex process of embodiment that correlates with the double function of construction, and also presents two interlaced facets. The first: the materialization of the body, the material constitution of the process as body, the transformation of the body through the process. The second: the phenomenal constitution of self and world, their appearance for the body as subject, the co-emergence for the embodied process of the mutually adapting enabling forces of the process as senseful—and beyond, perhaps, meaningful—presences.

Accepting this argumentation, it is a process of adaptation—and an adapting process—that encounters constructed matter now. It is a complex dynamic system that now gets in touch with constructed matter. Construction, thus, now intervenes in an ongoing dynamic system. It inexorably becomes part of the system in which it interferes as a new constraint.

This postulation, instead of approaching the situation on a threefold basis as I did before—body, surroundings, constructed surroundings—allows us to observe it as twofold—the dynamic system of embodiment and the intervening constructively organized matter—and eventually as one single complex, relational, dynamic unit—the system, which by virtue of the plasticity of one of its components, the body, is able to incorporate, to embody, the constructive variation of the body's environment.

Construction intervenes in the dynamics that connect the parts of the system. Considered now not as an alteration of one of its parts but autonomously, it does not directly alter these parts but the flow that joins them, the course of their mutual adaptation. It modulates the relationships configured by the reciprocity between the sensorimotor activity of the body and the activities of its surroundings that reach it.

It does not change the fundamental way in which these dynamics are organized. At least not immediately. It intervenes in the system without varying its basic regulation—the system is self-organized long before construction intervenes.

Instead, construction modifies the actual development of its dynamics, providing new possibilities. It enlarges the domain of their realization through introducing new constraints.

In one extreme case, construction blocks the communication between the parts of the system. At least for a while it completely breaks the unmediatedness of the connection between them. It blocks, it isolates, it disconnects, it disjoints.

A room without windows and doors. A perfect joining of thick surfaces—floor, walls, ceiling. In an even more drastic case, only one continuous surface, without joints. Without articulation. Disarticulated and disarticulating.
A surface completely surrounding the body. Simultaneously, inevitably, a surface completely surrounded by its original surroundings. A double aboveness facing all agents of the system. Dislocating them. Breaking the locus—the place, the conditions of possibility of its emergence.
An all-over barrier. A non-permeable membrane. An attack against the spontaneity of the system. A brutal interference against its constitutive dynamics, obstructing the medium of its development, inhibiting the connective agency of its members.

Nevertheless, blockage is not the end. Blockage leads to substitution, since it is fundamentally the inner dynamics of one component of the system—the body—that animates the whole, that induces the dynamics of the whole, that activates the potential agency of the surroundings. Its isolation, the reciprocal insulation of body and surroundings from one another, unavoidably turns construction into an island, the new surroundings of the body, the new agent for its actualization. The new partner in the con-versation—the continuous fluctuation towards and against one another.
And based on this substitution the case can be sharpened, reducing the articulation of this new partner in different ways. Reducing even more

the differences, the potential eloquence of this new interlocutor.
Monochrome surface(s). Only one material. Dismembering the new
surroundings. Minimizing their affordances, suffocating their appeal.
Or reducing their dimensions. Restraining the development of the
motoric potentialities of the body.
Or reducing the reflectivity of the surfaces, changing their single
color and single material to absorb any kind of light or sound, to keep
them from the body, thus repressing the actualization of its sensory
potentiality.
An anechoic chamber, an absolutely dark room. No response, no reflection, no resonance. No possible perceptual constitution—no form.
An isolation cell. Total disorientation.
Surroundings as vacuum. Radical re-duction of the new surrounding as
the leading-back of the body to the no-body. To its death.

The intervention of construction can on the contrary enhance the connecting dynamics of the system. It can facilitate the expansion of the
motoric domain of the body.
A path, a bridge, a ramp. Steps, stairs, a platform. A combination of
platforms connected by paths, bridges, ramps, steps, stairs. Or simply
disposed close to each other, accessible to the body without further
connecting elements.
Extension of the surroundings in both dimensions. Allowing the body
to go further, to go higher or lower. To cross. To be over, to be sustained. In different ways. In new, perhaps unknown and unexpected
ways. To navigate in ways not facilitated by the unaltered surroundings
but by their constructive alteration, by their constructed extension.

By virtue of their mutually determining interlacement, the potential
extension of the motoric made possible through construction implies
possible expansions of the sensory. The possibilities of new perspectives. Of taking a new position in relation to the agency of the surroundings, new positions for new potential forms of adaptation—for

touching and being touched in different ways, from different angles, in and from divergent directions. Of sounding out new possible encounters. Renewed, revisited encounters.

Changes in the materiality of the constructive elements, for example in their degree of opacity, enable further modulations. To see under our feet—a translucent platform, a semi-opaque path, a transparent bridge. To confront, to experience simultaneously our sense of stability, of solidity, of carrying and loading capacity, of trust to be sustained, supported, and underpinned, and to see through to and access the other side—the side usually occluded in order to allow me to do what we are nevertheless doing now—to be exposed to what is beyond and otherwise not actually present. The simultaneous and thus, at least for an initial moment, conflictive presence of hitherto dislocated and even incompatible senses leads to a crisis, to a chance for the diversification of the domain of relationships, of modes of interaction between body and surroundings, and consequently of their presences—of their forms and significances—for the subject modulated by these new interactions.

Blockage and enhancement open up a field of perhaps infinite varieties of interferences in the systemic dynamics that articulate the structural coupling of bodies and surroundings through construction. A field between the dark, absorbing, minute, closed room and the stable bridge overcoming the insurmountable gap.

Introducing fissures into the closeness, the impermeability, progressively allowing the contact, the communication, the touch, the response. Or, starting from the opposite extreme, limiting the empowering surfaces, materializing their limits, elevating them, constructing the emptiness that begins where they end. Joining a path, just wide enough to walk alone, with a wall, higher than my head, at a ninety-degree angle. Being able to walk safely, feeling a reinforced and leveled

support under my feet, but now, simultaneously, the invitation to move forward in only one direction, feeling a partial, subtle restriction of my possibility to turn caused by the limited horizontal surface and the solidification of one of its limits through a vertical plane.
Introducing resistance. Reinforcing potential vectors. Inducing their actualization, their realization.
Partially compressing a flow. Laterally. Edgewise. Providing conditions for an intensified presence of the body's chirality. Enhancing asymmetry. Facilitating its unmediated presence through the mediation of this simple construction.
Dividing. Partially restricting the agency of the surroundings and simultaneously increasing the autonomy of their constructive modification. Making a triality plausible. Revealing the duality through the simultaneity of the potential extension and restraint of its terms.

Now adding a third constructive element. Two simple possibilities, two ways of repeating the same operation—the addition of another surface, again in a nineteen-degree relationship. The first, joining the vertical with a new horizontal situating a surface above my head—which would implement compression, increase division, restriction, and further reinforce the autonomous presence of the increasingly present third agent, the constructed surrounding. Solidity above the body where there was nothing but an infinite space. Nothing coming from where there had once been incessant changes. Stabilization, pressure, numbness. The bringing-about of self-referentiality.

The second possible extension of the construction: to join another wall to the opposite edge of the path. Another variety of compression, this time lateral. Now reinforcing symmetry. Fostering movement on a straight line. Promoting its unidirectionality. Potentiating its velocity, its acceleration as a possible way to transform, to conduct the increased pressure on the body. As a way of canalizing it, of letting it pass by passing faster.
Simultaneously, if the walls and the floor are hard, opaque, and polished, the arising of reflections. Repetitions—we would say, explaining

the phenomena outside of its unmediated experience—that do not necessary appear as such but rather, aurally, as a qualitative modification and extension of durations—resonance—and, visually, as my own presence, or to be more precise, as a new presence—a reflection—that I sooner rather than later accept as or attribute to my-self. A self I could rarely receive, retake from my non-constructed surroundings. Only under precise conditions—as is well known, when I face completely still water, when it acquires the solidity of the walls I am facing now.

When reflection happens in both sensory modes simultaneously, the disruption induced by construction manifests as such—as divergence, as disagreement—in the otherwise coherent sphere of the sensuous. Reflection leads, here already, to separation, to disconnection, to analysis. Aurally, the presences of my environment and of myself disjoin. The first becomes vague, distant, altered in its inner structure—heavier, fuzzier, shadowy. The second, contrastingly, is reinforced. The body becomes a producer of auditory presence. Movement spontaneously becomes sound before it can be produced deliberately. I become a sounding presence for myself. I become sound to myself—aural reflection. Visually, if the surfaces are opaque and polished, the outside disappears. Or better said the outside appears—as outside. The outside is established now—excluded from where I am, excluding me from where it is becoming. There is an inaccessible zone, a clear division beyond the distinction of different topological qualities. There is now an area on and incipiently in which I am. And another one. Without me. Simultaneously, looking at the walls, facing the surfaces facing me—not the others outside—a new "mine" emerges interlaced with this arising self. This my-self I begin to see from my outside in this inside. In an unmediated manner, facing it directly, without speculating about my otherness on the basis of the otherness of others-for-my-self but rather coming back to the original speculation—observing, con-templating, interacting with this new area, this incipient temenos.

Now joining the two options we have been exploring separately: a path, two walls on its edges and a surface parallel to the path bridging the walls on their upper ends. In addition to the reinforcement of the presences that have been emerging in each phase of this exploration, there is now a new presence, which—we can say now, when it fully appears— has already been partially, incipiently present: the exclusive presence of only one piece of the non-constructed surroundings "at the end of" or perhaps "beyond" the cuboid construction. Those that were all around the body—an all-over presence for the subject they enabled, its complete, continuous environment. Those that were there every time, because they were everywhere. Now, having been restrained and transformed into a possible outside—while the body has been constrained and situated in a potential inside—a section of this outside acquires a certain autonomy—from the all-over surroundings and even from the body that, now, faces it—turning into "a view." A singularization in and of the process of viewing, a temporary stabilization, a contoured visual presence—an objectification. A transitory detention, a stop, a hold that perhaps induces the body to stop as well, as it did before, perhaps, to contemplate itself on the inner face of a wall, but this time not moved by the reflecting agency of the polished surfaces but by virtue of their capacity to frame.

The presence of this objectified piece of the surroundings, its new, solid quality, which allows it to be thrown in front of the body—to be ob-ject-ified—counteracts the movement, the acceleration that the compression of the tunnel exerts on the body. Two counteracting forces that find their counterpart in the performance of the sensorimotor potency of the body.

It stops. Maybe it sits down. To look. To look at this thisnness the body can now point to—it probably points to its center, to this section of the section, to this thisnness inside of this thisnness, a particularity in the particular.

Simultaneously and mutually constituted con-centration. Facilitated by the combination of two varieties of constructive agency—blocking and enabling.

The body stops and projects. It acquires a new quality of steadiness facing the new steadiness of its former dynamic, all-over surroundings, and pro-jects—a new combination of movement and non-movement. It performs a new quality of sensory activity. It throws-out—its sight, its attention, itself—towards that what is now thrown-in-front, even thrown-against it—its ob-ject-ified surroundings. In projecting, the body learns a new, perhaps even more intimate, more in-tense variety of touch—intensified due to its necessity to stretch-towards the new object, to that section of what was undivided, to what was so close it could not even be touched. A new variety of in-tentionality, a new way to refer, to tend-towards its surrounding. A new manner of con-nec-tion—of binding-together. A new way of contributing to the interplay of coupled and coupling agencies, which the body had somehow, already performed before it got in touch with construction, tended towards the single components of its surroundings—to their spontan-eously singularized areas, to those objects involuntarily constituted, passively synthesized through perception, to the things it had always been meeting out there.

Now, due to the body's interaction with the agency generated by the constructive alteration of its surroundings, these surroundings—the whole they were—become a part. They are singularized, constituted as a singular, contoured entity. A view, an image, a land-scape—a created, cut, scraped, shaped, land. An object, somehow, like the objects that the body had met before, those singular presences that appear to be given to the subject but to the constitution of which the subject con-tributes through its bodiness, through the process of embodiment it shares with its surroundings. Like now, when it stops, sits down—sur-rounded by its new surroundings—and directs its sight towards its for-mer and still—but now differently so—actual surroundings, which now, due to the synchronic actualization of the agencies of body and con-struction, becomes a view, a vista, a scenery, an incipient land-scape.

Or now, when stopping, the body attends, stretches-towards the aural presences that appear constrained by this specific construction with which it now interacts—with which it now becomes it-self. Actions of the components of its surrounding now occurring "on the other side" of the walls with which they in-form—or better, con-form—what now reaches the body, what now touches it.

Or interacting with the open frame in front of it, towards which it is now looking, pointing.

Two situations, dynamically connected to one another. The first, when the body is in touch with the activities of its surroundings-on-the-other-side aurally but possibly without having visual contact with the acting things. The second, when the visual presence of the vibrating things temporarily cross the now restricted field of visual contact between the body and its now framed surroundings "out there." In any case, a disjunction of what used to be a unity. An actualization of the potential division between sensory modes, and therefore a potentiation of each mode as a single and singular one. "I hear but I don't see"—"what I hear," we would say, actually meaning "what vibrates allowing me to hear." A reinforcement of the possible autonomy of hearing, of seeing. Of the possibilities to con-centrate on singular modalities of sensuous presences, of focusing—with the vibrating, reflecting, resonating actors—on singular kinds of shared activity. Concentrating, thus, on the aural now, framing becomes filtering. A complex process of filtering—simultaneously letting past, blocking and reinforcing. Letting certain ranges of vibration pass, blocking others—leaving them "outside," where, as we will later discover, we can meet them again, when we "go back" to this disappearing-outside, this disappearing-as-outside. And reinforcing other areas of these new aural presences that, as we hear now, become divisible, differentiated, revealing their own interiority—revealed through this interiority in which—with which—we now are.

A twofold moment of aural singularization. On the one hand, the singularization of the sound presences as such, as differentiated from the vibrating things, especially if "we don't know what that is" when we begin to look for it—increasing our aural attentiveness, scrutinizing the singularized presence as well as the recalled presence of former sounds, trying to re-member, to articulate through re-cognition, through a re-configuration of the unity between aural objects and vibrating things. Or trying to overcome the visual blockage, moving towards the opening, towards the space of visual re-connection with what is now the outside, with what was, simply, our surroundings. Aural presence as pure aural presence, disconnected from its material correlate.

On the other hand a singularization of certain sections of the singularized sounds. In turn, a difference that can become present in a twofold way. A rather analytical one, which presents the single sounds as complex phenomena, intrinsically composed of the coalescence of the areas we are now able to differentiate easily, due to their reinforced presence or their absence. "Low sections," "high sections," "middle sections," we can say, spontaneously structuring the all-over, fuzzy presence in a dimension we use for ourselves as bodies or for the construction surrounding us. Or addressing this difference in a synthetic way, singularizing the aural presence as a whole, as a different presence—different from the one we know, the one we have heard "outside." A new manifestation of the difference between inside and outside, which aurally reinforces this distinction on the basis of a re-cognition of the sound and implicitly of the reestablishment of the unity between the sound and the vibrating thing. "Here it sounds different," we could say. "It sound lower, deeper, blunter, duller." "An interior sound," we could also come to say, or even, referring instead to where we are through our aural experience, "Now I am inside."

An endless investigation. Infinite possibilities of the organization of matter, of the constructive modification of the body's surroundings, of modulating their agency through construction, of actualization through constructing their potentiality to block and to enable. Inexhaustible ways of interfering through construction in the dynamic coupling between body and surroundings, of simultaneously constraining their mutually constraining agencies.

Unlimited ways of organizing matter through constructively modifying its agency, providing new, unexpected options for the body to lay down its path, to challenge the plasticity of its own organization, which enables the whole process of embodiment to take place—to become simultaneously place and subject.

A subject gets in touch with architectural construction. Deliberately organized matter that interferes now, inevitably, in its process of becoming-subject—of becoming-subject-with-its-environment. Regarding one of the interlaced dynamics that constitute this complex process—taking a perspective of observation for us now, writing/reading, not being this emerging subject but observing it—we could say that a body—"the body of the subject," we would tend to say spontaneously, expressing the cognitive paradigm we are trying to escape—the subject-body, the body-becoming-subject, the body being embodied by its becoming subject and becoming subject through its embodiment, now gets in touch with an alteration of its surroundings. The selfness of the body, this emerging embodied self, carries on its relational processes of becoming it-self now in interaction with new constraints, with new agencies of the surrounding matter enabled by its constructive organization.

By virtue of this alteration, the body modifies its relational operativity. It con-ducts it-self in different ways. It navigates its altered, perhaps expanded operative domain in new ways, adapting anew, elaborating new actualizations of its own potentialities.
New varieties of viability—new ways of maintaining the coupling with its surroundings through which it becomes the self it is becoming.

New viabilities through new coherences—new potential paths to cross the newly emerging environment. New coherences through new viabilities—new ways to cohere, which are confirmed, sustained, reinforced, again and again, with every new step.

Potential valences, latent vectors that emerge, that become, cautiously, actualized—embodied. Incipient significances. Inchoate tendencies.

Destabilizations of habitualized ways to proceed—of sedimented sensorimotor patterns—giving rise, gradually, to new possible stabilizations. Germinal phenomena. Not yet phenomena but their intimately interlaced processes of becoming. Not yet present as phenomena but operatively—immanently, in each new tentative step along the new, subtle paths that are now being laid down by new ways of walking—of walking with constructed matter.

Not yet contoured presences. Not yet formalized, objectified. Not yet configured enough to be manifest, to appear as differentiated from the dense woven processes that cause them to become themselves—themselves for the subject with which and to which they are being constituted. Not yet new expressions of objectifying intentionality. Not yet new configurations produced by this variety of aboutness that singularizes, that differentiates this from that—that informs different thisnesses out of a continuous dynamic ground. That points, that cuts, that demarcates.

Immanent presences. Presences that are not yet differentiated from the processual meshwork of relations in which they are coming to be. Remaining, still, operative. Embodying, in a very subtle way—in movement, as sensible movement—this other variety of aboutness, this attention to the whole dynamic system as a whole in which these presences emerge. Performing—achieving-form-through—operative intentionality.

Radical immanency. Subtle, vague, dynamic, intrinsic presences allowing phenomena to be trans-formed, to overcome their stabilized forms, their habitualized significances in favor of new, perhaps unexpected ones.

Constructive interference giving rise to new relational states, to new states of the dynamic coupling between the body-becoming-subject and surroundings-becoming-its-environment. To new situations—new embodiments, new emplacements.
And beyond, on this unstable basis, to new per-ceptual and con-ceptual presences—new ways of grasping what is fleeting, what is fleeing, what is passing—by passing through in different ways.

New stabilizations, new demarcations. Renewed phenomena. New components of our own stability, of our orientation, of our most fundamental identity, and simultaneously of the identity of the place we are in—we are with.
"I am here." So just. Anew. Again. And again. "I am inside," perhaps. "I am entering," "I am protected," or maybe, "I am exposed." Or simply, "I have to leave," following a clear though inexplicit sense of inadequacy, of mutual rejection, or perhaps the attraction of the "outside," the renewed presence of this otherness enabled by the construction that has co-constituted this new thisness in and with which I now am—I am becoming this renewed I in this renewed here.

An inextricable and, with analytical procedures, inscrutable network of silent varieties of coupling between the body and its surrounding, of ways in which their agencies spontaneously adapt, reinvent their interlacements, cohere anew.
New ways for the body to encounter, to navigate its new surroundings that in-form them as a newly defined environment, as a new all-over senseful presence for the body-becoming-subject. Different forms of viability in a differing composition—a divergently constituted world-around.

Construction constraining the way sense emerges. The manner in which the subject finds ways through its environment, the way in which the viability-of-the-environment-for-the-subject appears—implicitly, operatively—to the subject.

Construction conditioning the very specific ways in which the all-over coherent presence around the subject appears to this subject as viable, as possible to be transited without imperiling the co-herence that holds both—subject and environment—together. As possible to be lived.

Moreover, construction—certain constructions—can accomplish an additional cognitive function, intimately connected with its more fundamental and generic one—it can constrain embodiment. Construction—certain constructions—can facilitate another kind of contact to the process of co-emergence of the subject and its environment, and, as one aspect of this process, of the ways in which the environment appears as viable for the subject.

Specific forms of organized matter can induce a kind of awareness of the mutual transitions between operative and perceptual/conceptual presences, between the processes of phenomenal (re)constitution and the constituted phenomena. They can compel a kind of conduct that, for the con-ducting and con-ducted body-becoming-subject, increases the transparency of its own con-duct.

A kind of conduct that allow us to see—vaguely, subtly, intimately, silently— "not only what words mean, but also the core of primary meaning round which the acts of naming and expression take shape" (Maurice Merleau-Ponty, Phenomenology of Perception, 1962, p. xvii).

sound essay,
video essay, and
research seminar

http://www.architecture-embodiment.org/transientsenses/sound-essay

This sound essay was presented for the first time at the Fundació Antoni Tàpies together with the video and text essays. It was reproduced through headphones AKG 271 MK II, which were also used for the recordings and the edition process.

video essay

http:// www. architecture-em bodiment.org/ transient senses/ **video-essay**

This video essay was presented for the first time at the Fundació Antoni Tàpies together with the sound and text essays. It was reproduced on a LED TV 55″ full HD screen. The file format has been modified in order to facilitate the streaming.

research seminar.
a video documentary

http://
www.
architecture-em
bodiment.org/
transient senses/
research-seminar

Directed by Adrià Sunyol and Natalia Alzate
Camera by Jordi Papasey and Paolo Giron
Sound by Oriol Campi

The research seminar took place at the Barcelona Pavilion, the Goethe
Institute in Barcelona, the Fundació Antoni Tàpies, and in the venue
of Sónar+D with the participation of Susanne Hauser, Dieter Mersch,
Gerard Vilar, Rudolf Bernet, Jean-Paul Thibaud, and Xavier Bassas,
and was moderated by Lluís Nacenta.

photographs

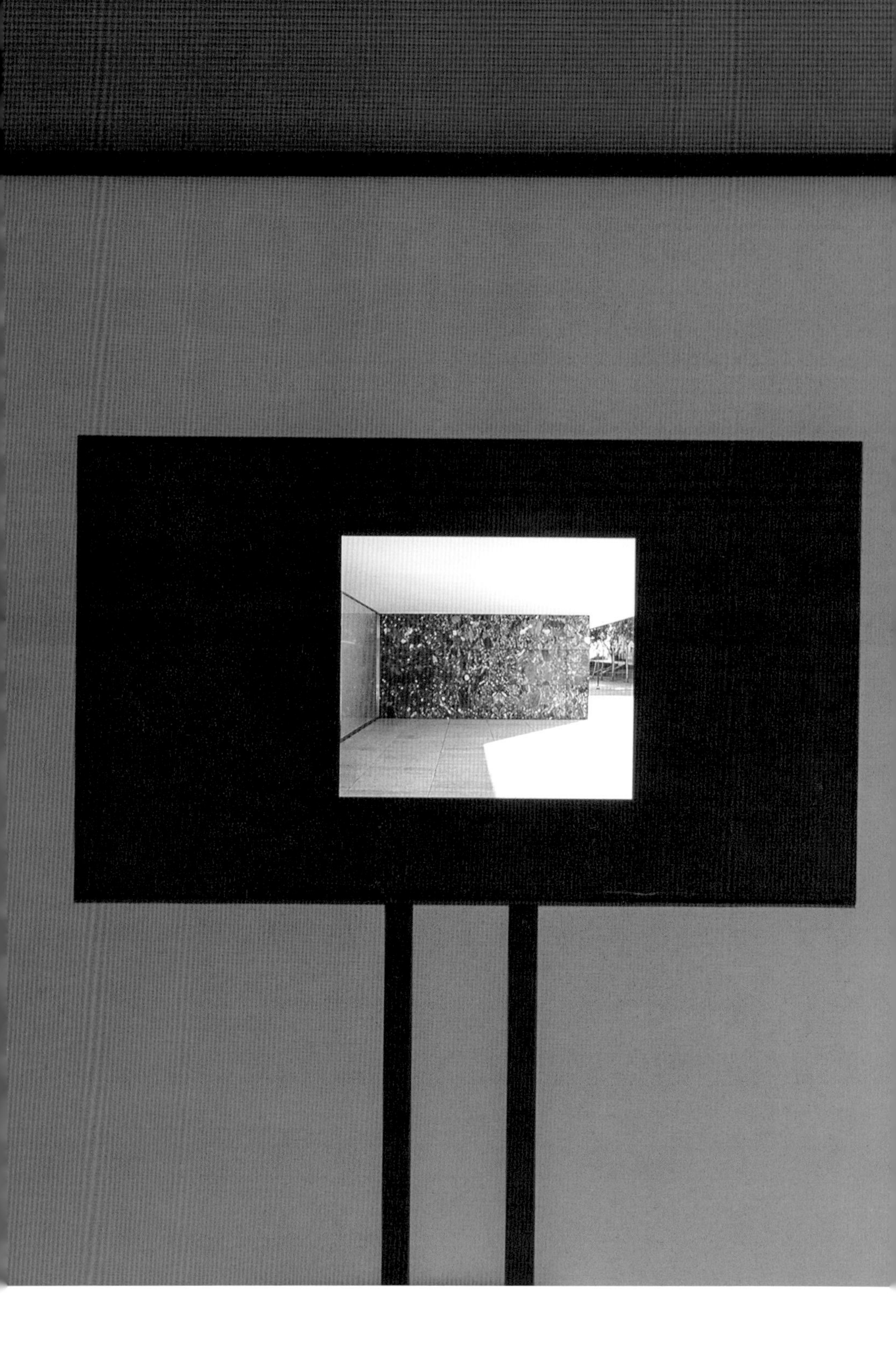

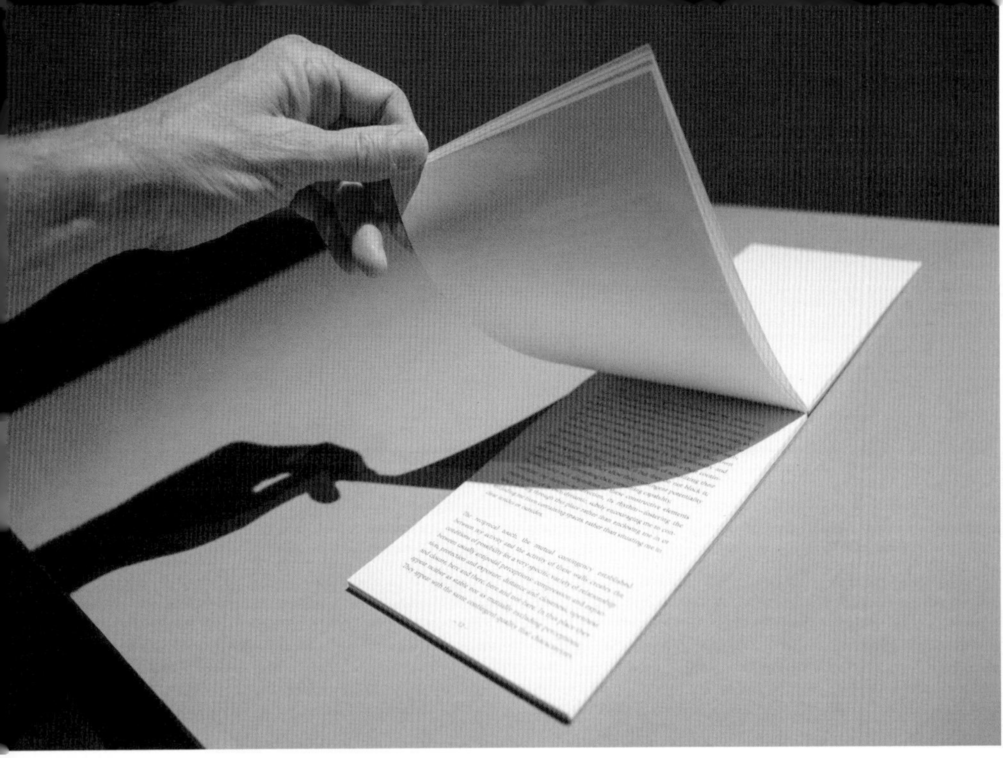

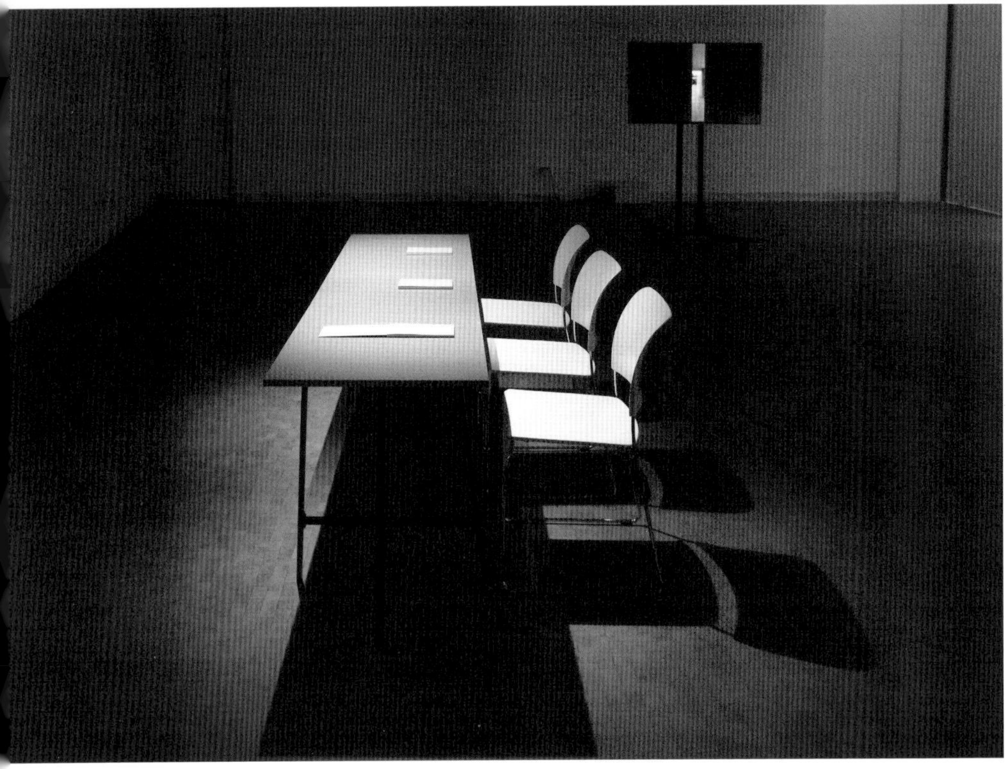

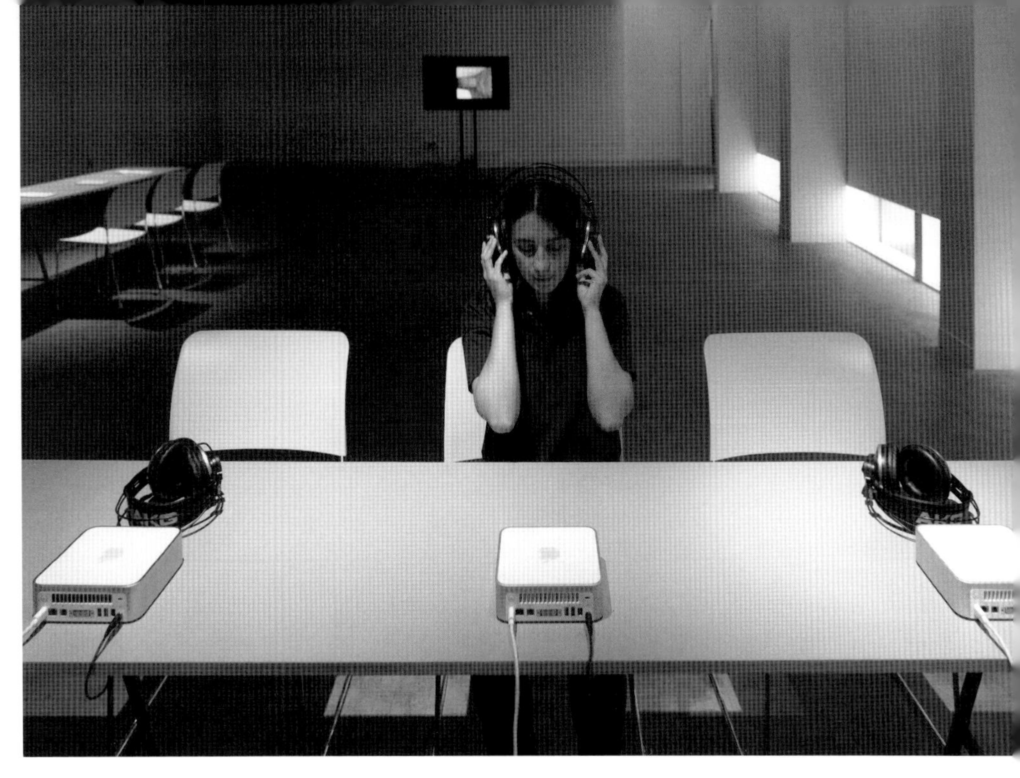

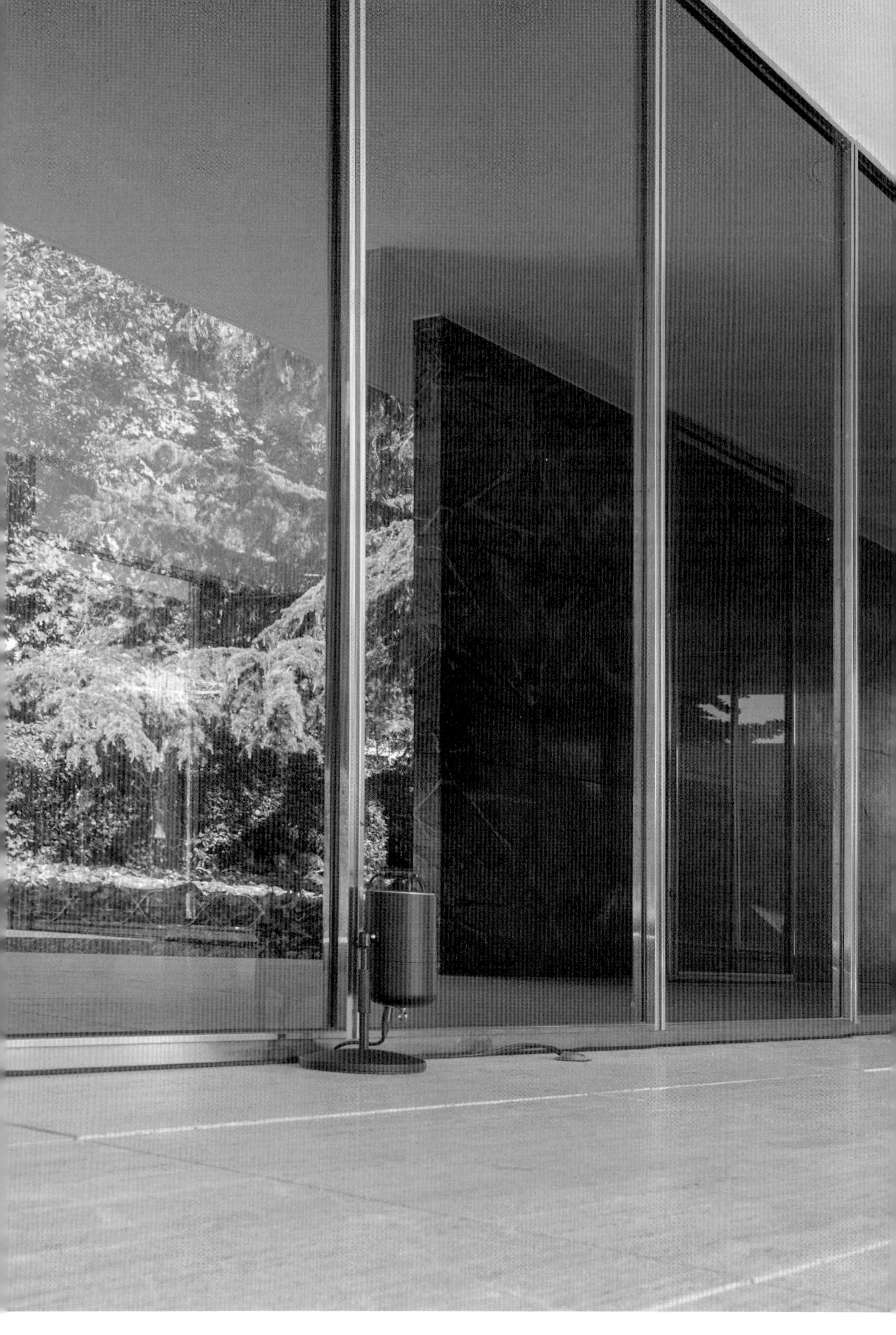

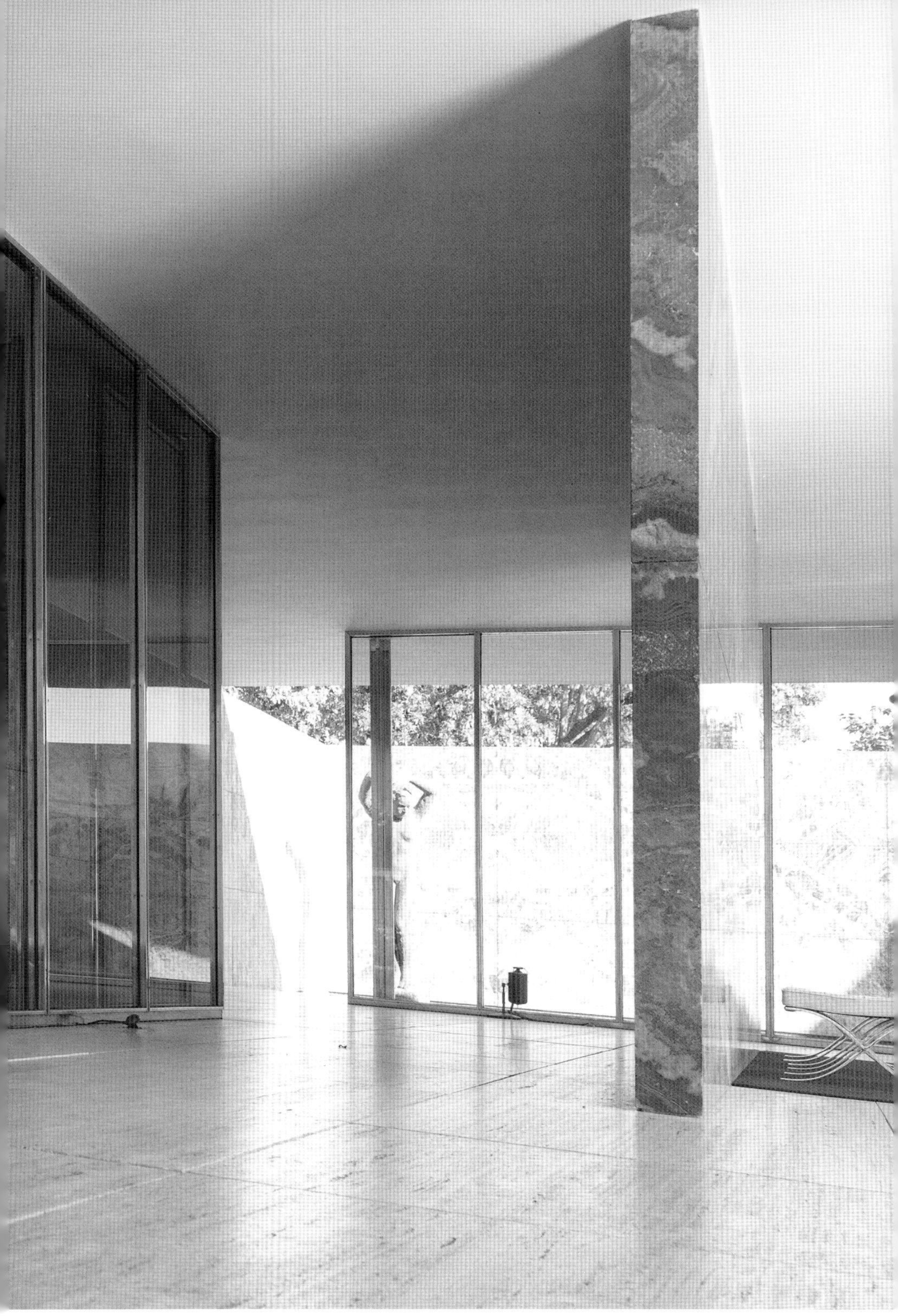

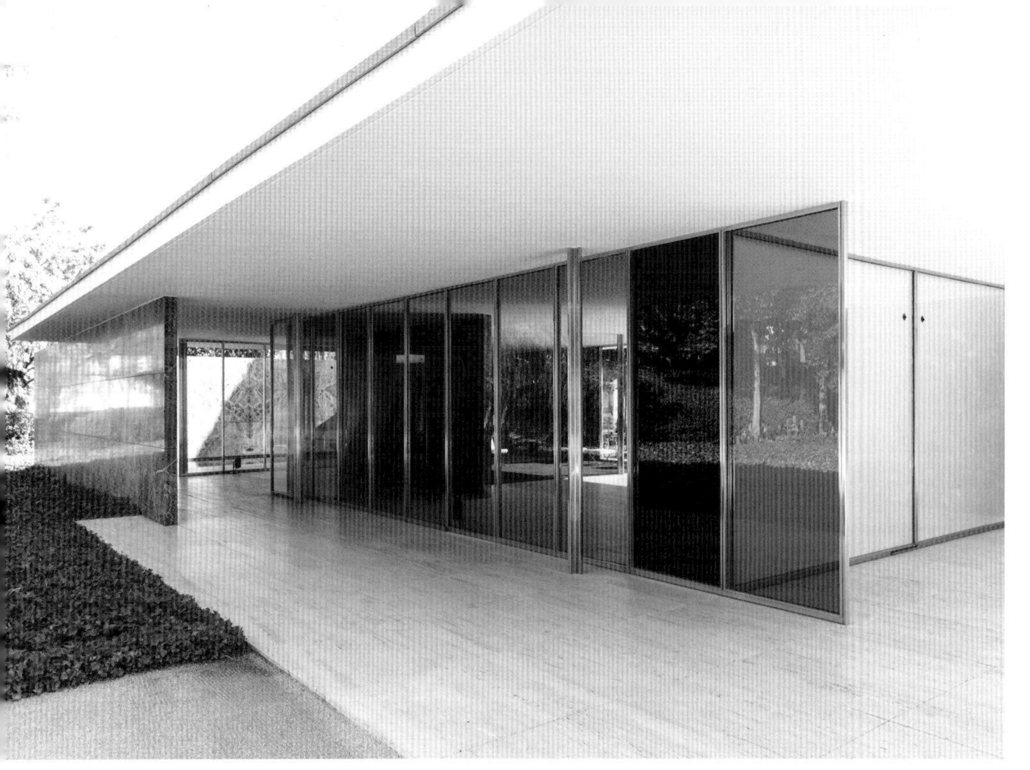

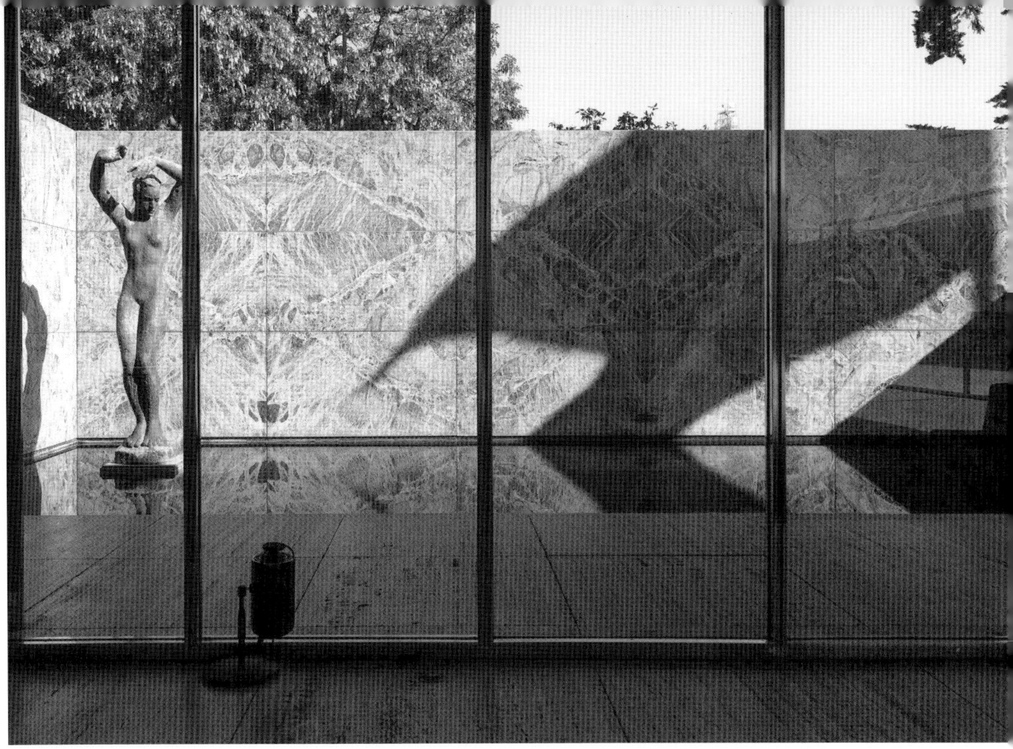

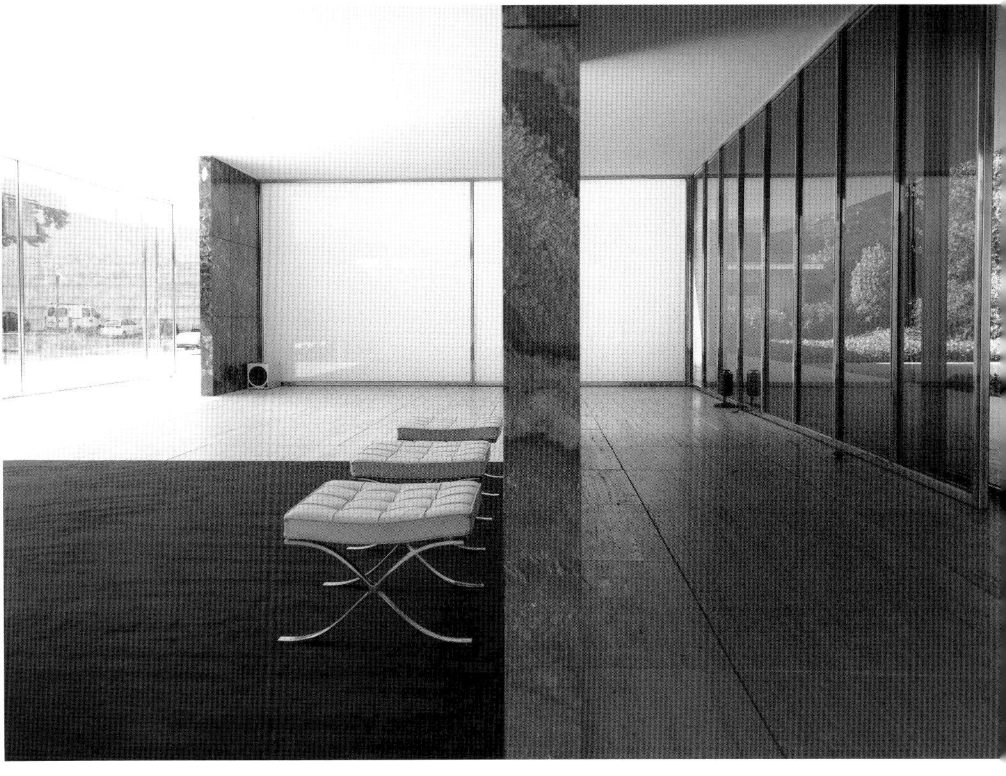

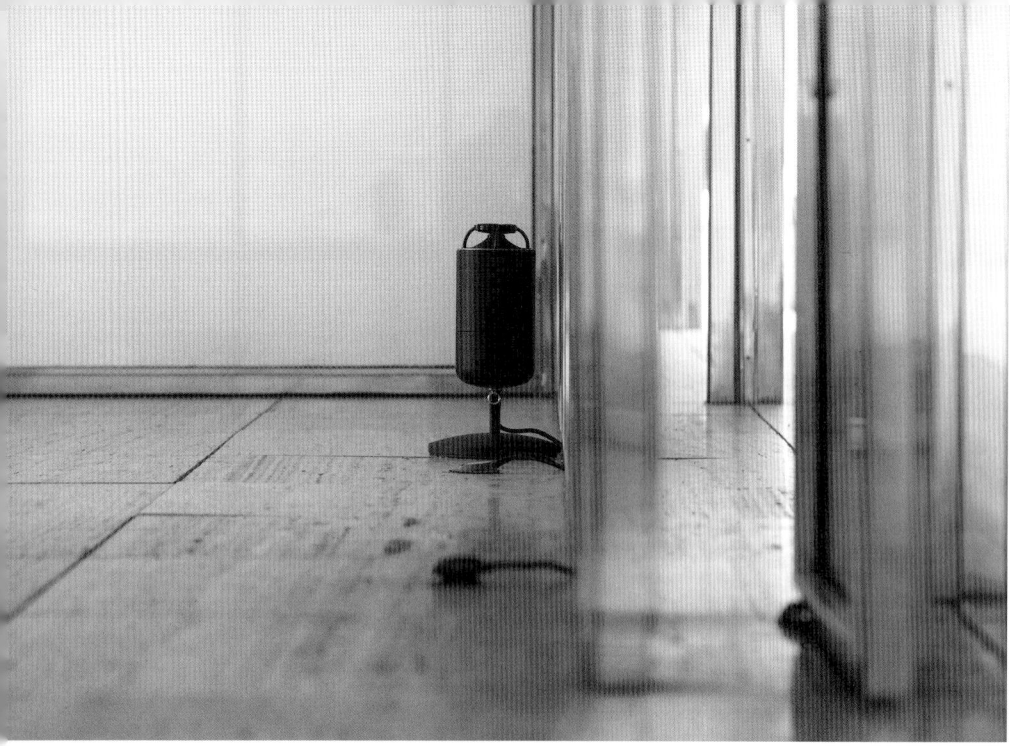

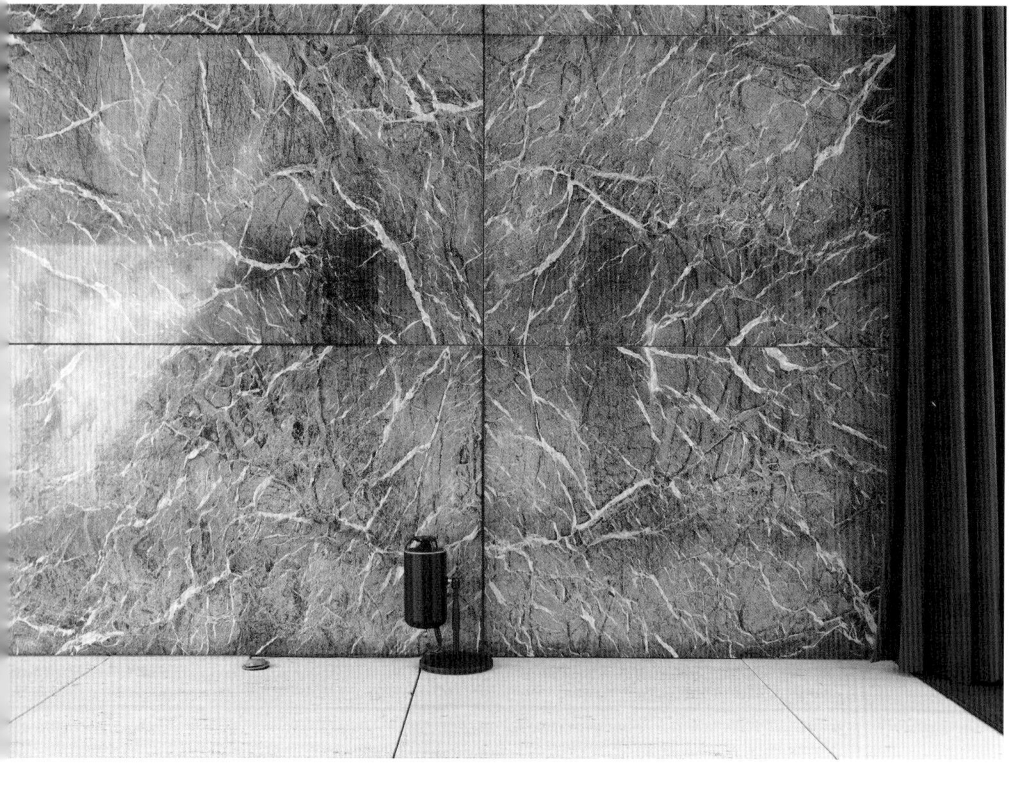

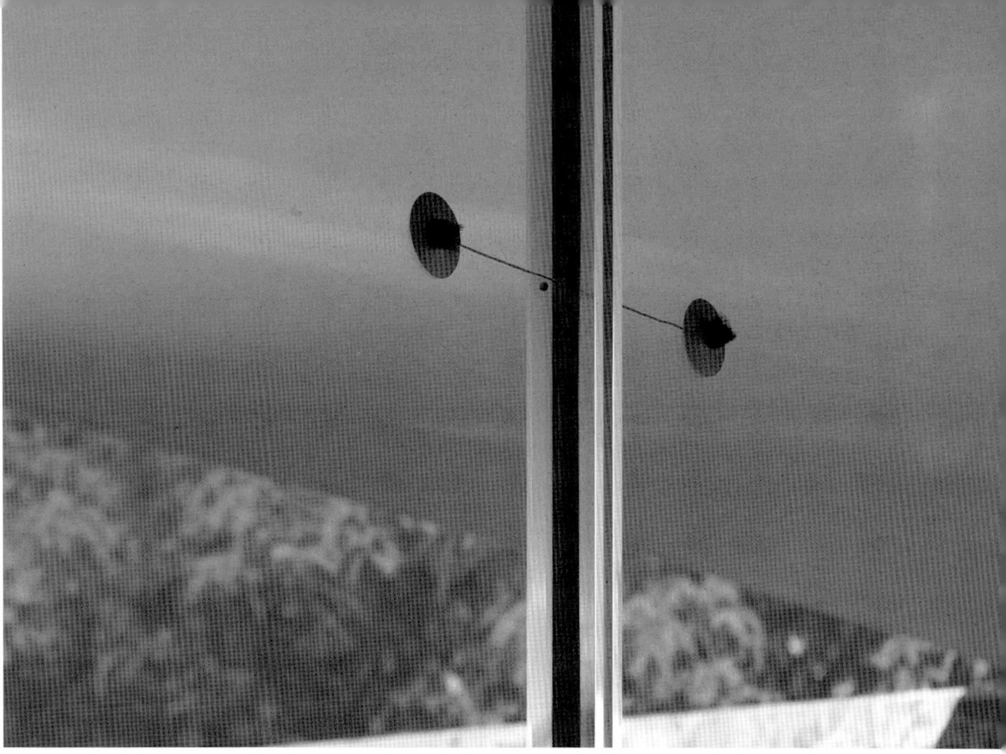

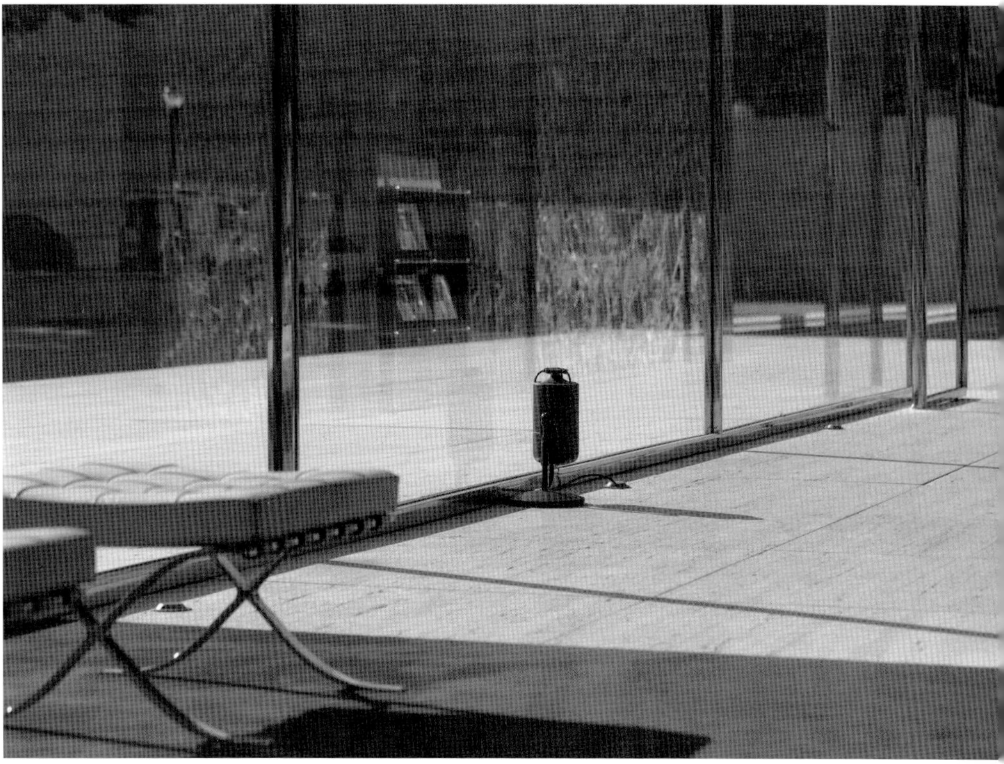

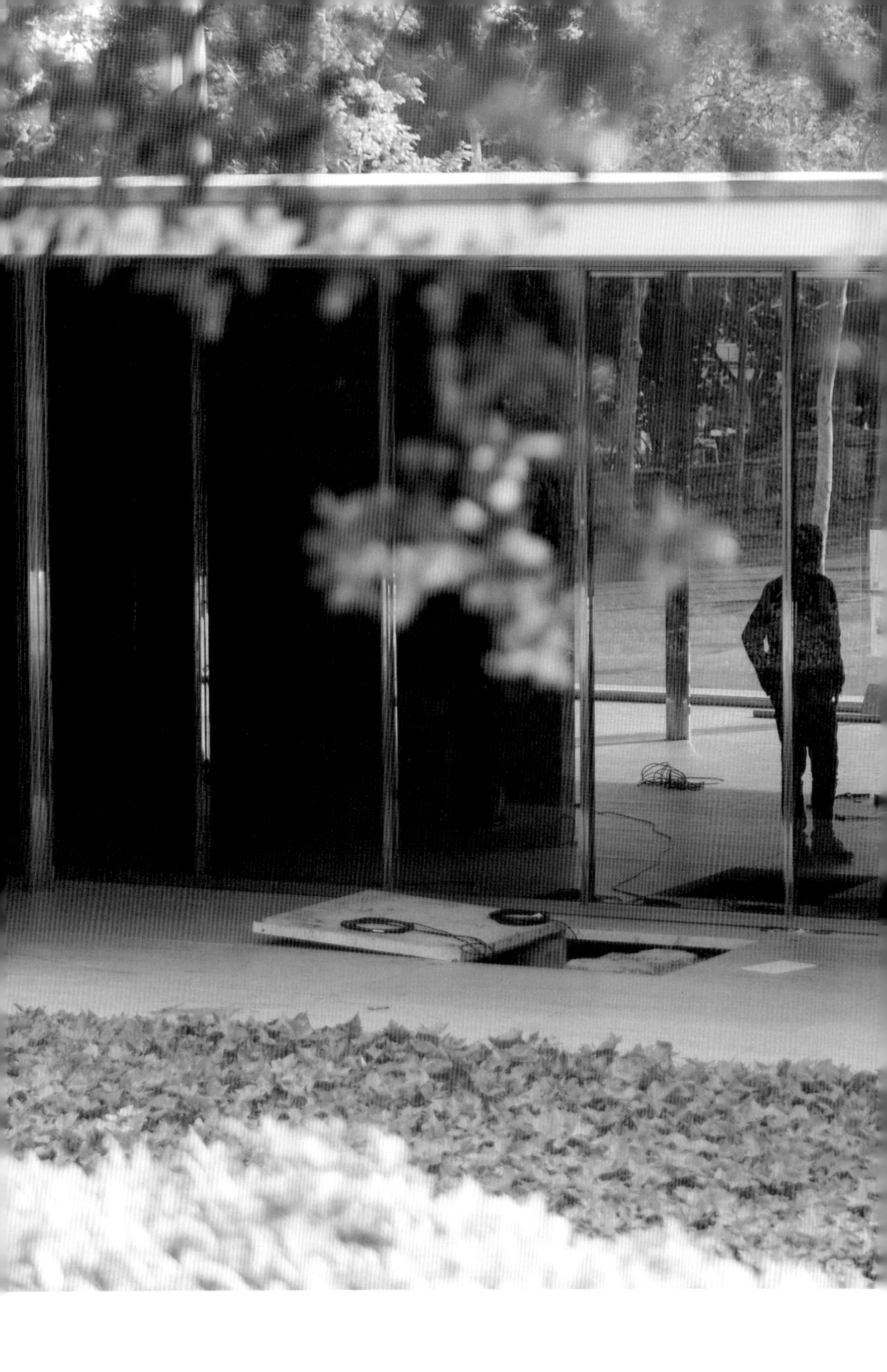

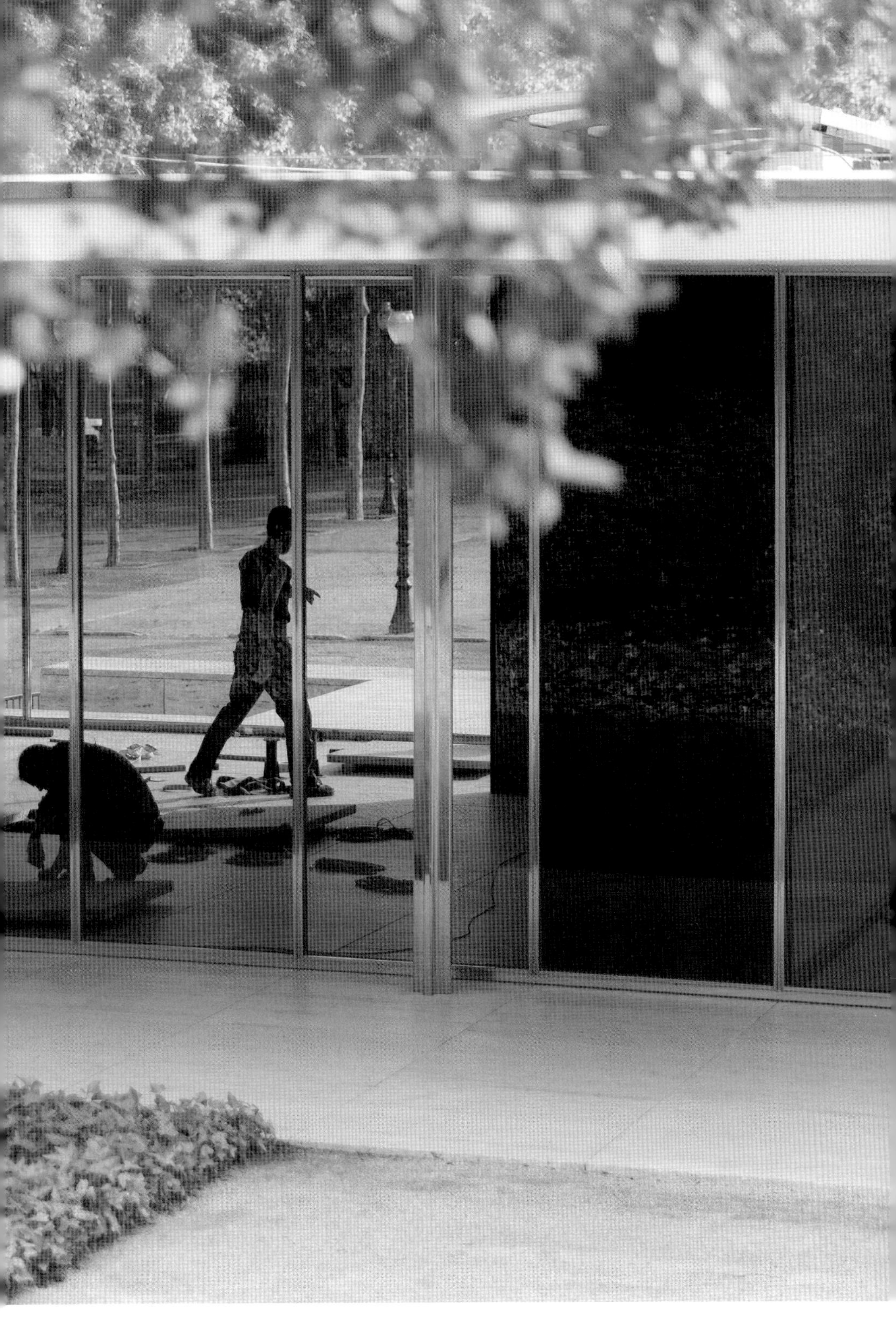

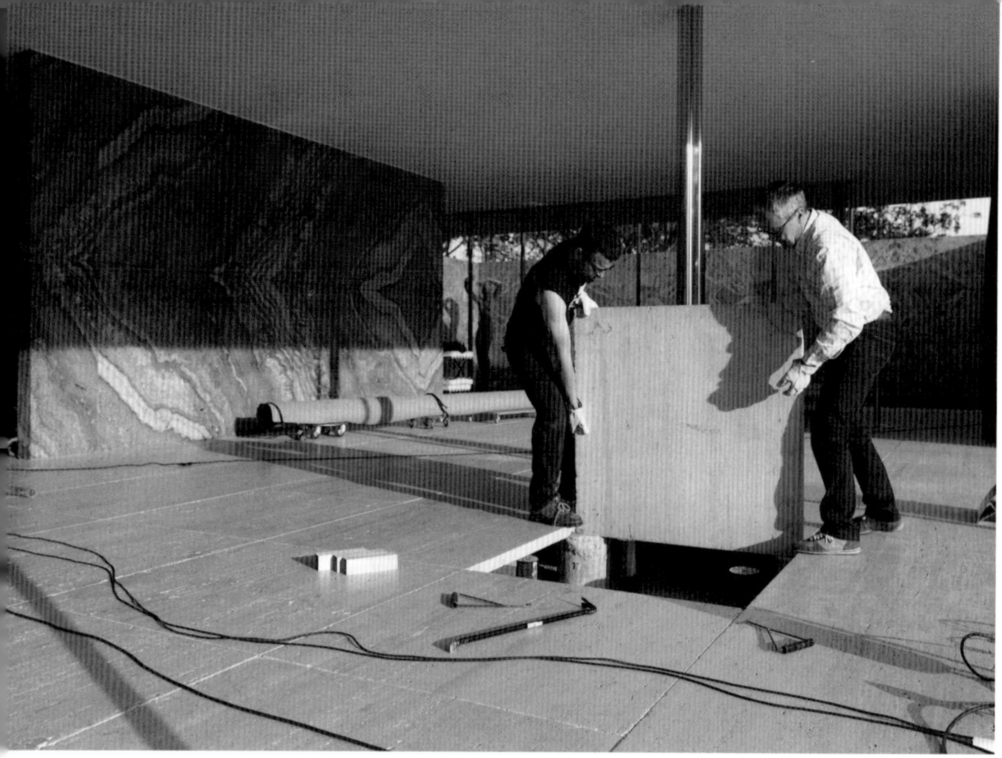

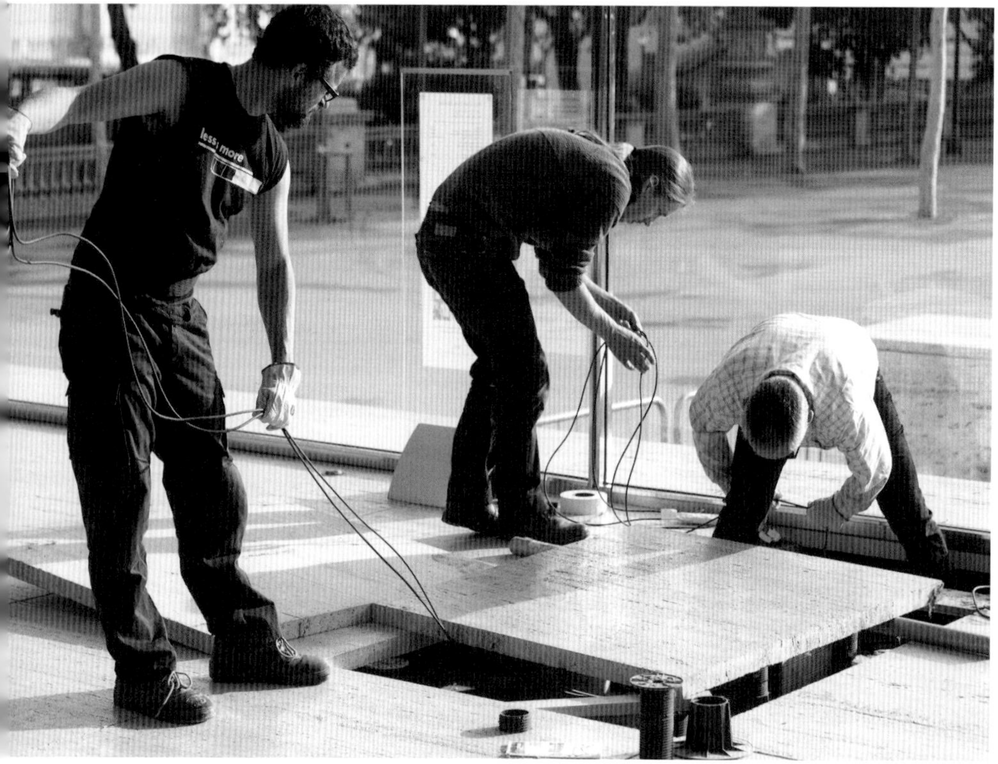

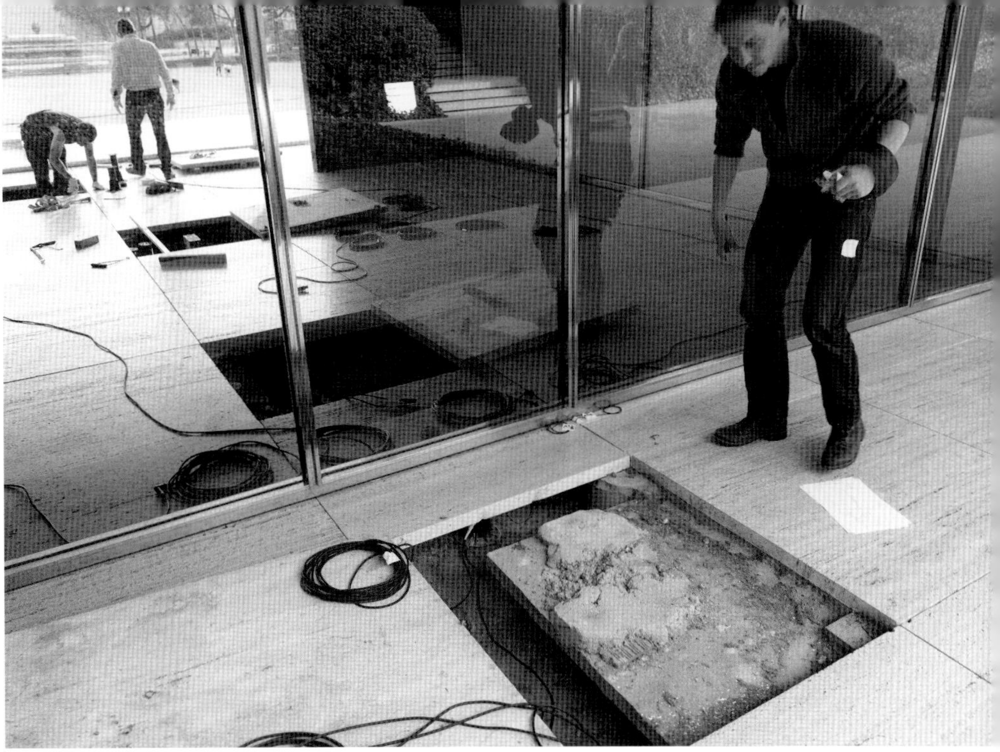

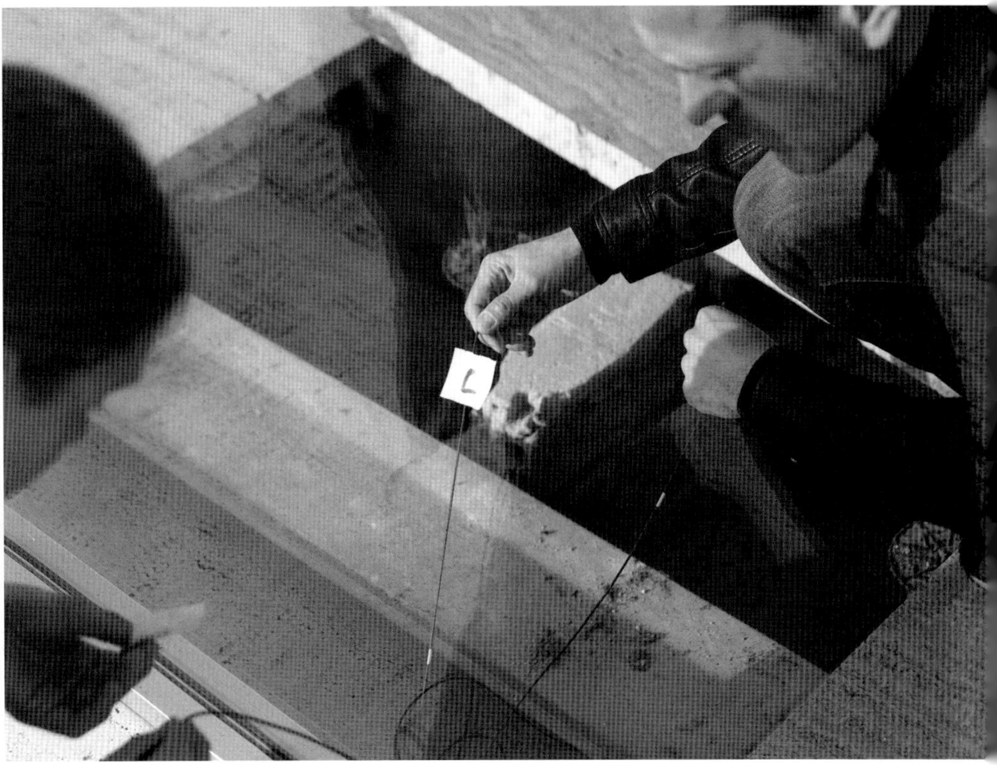

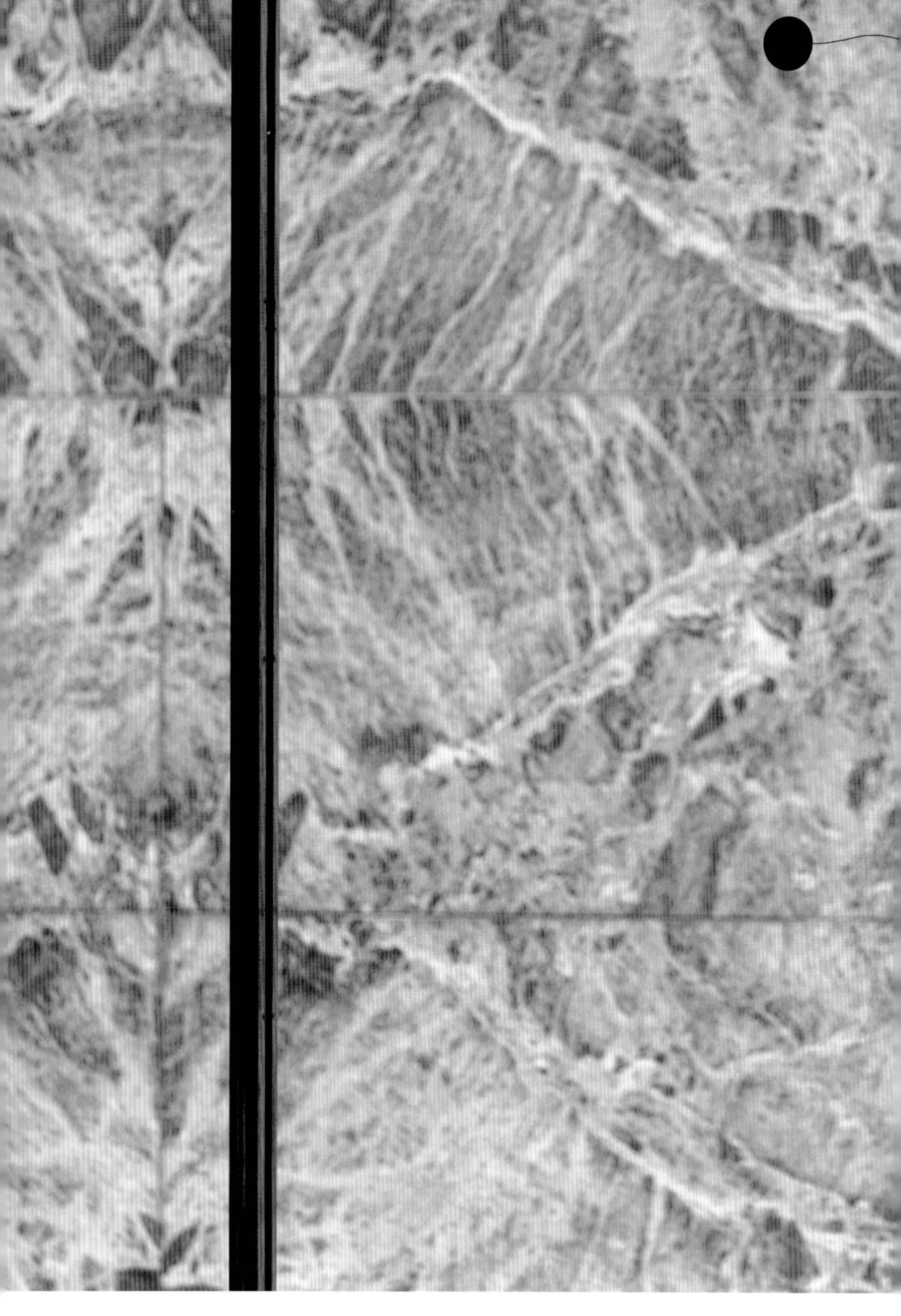

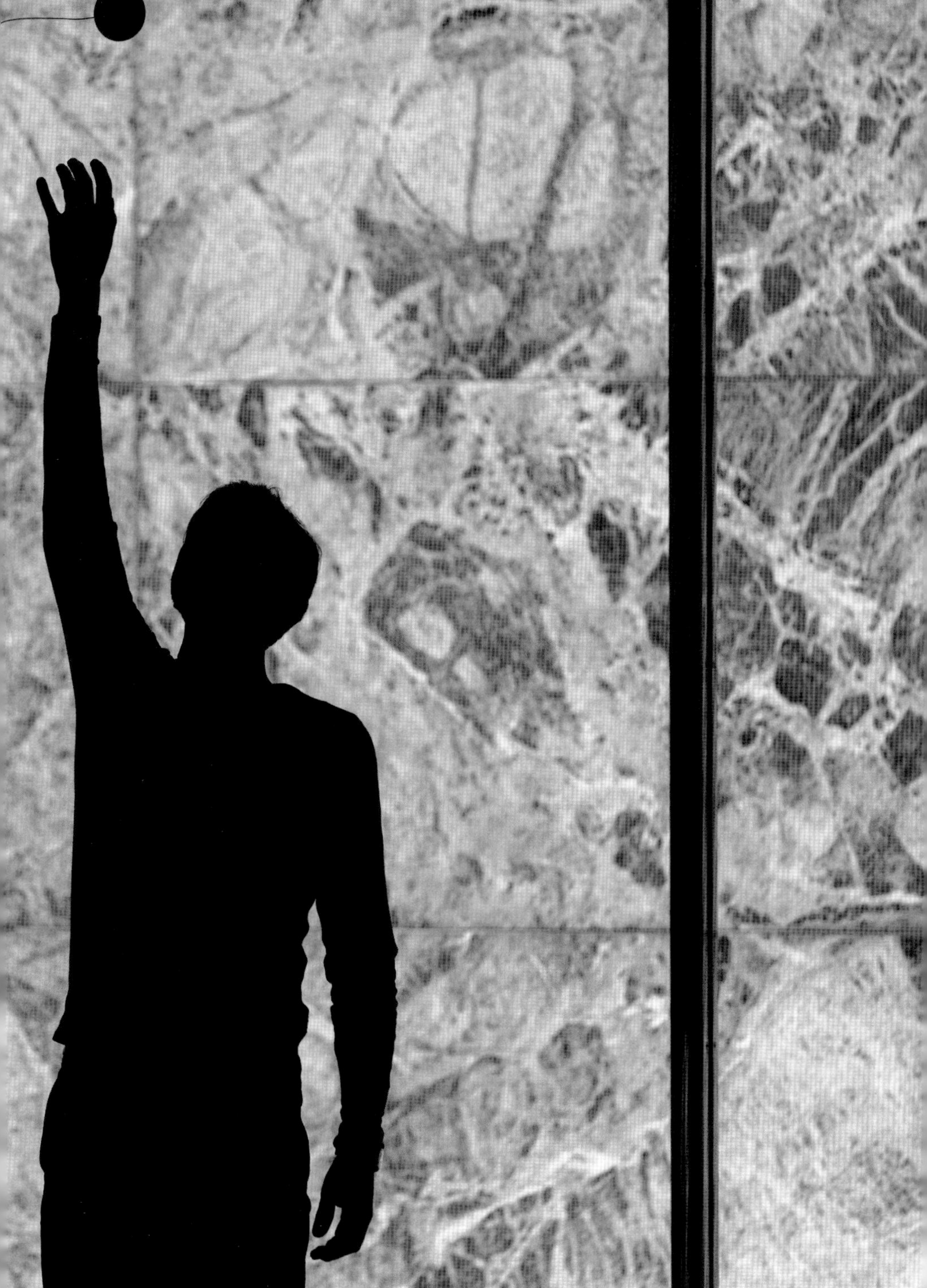

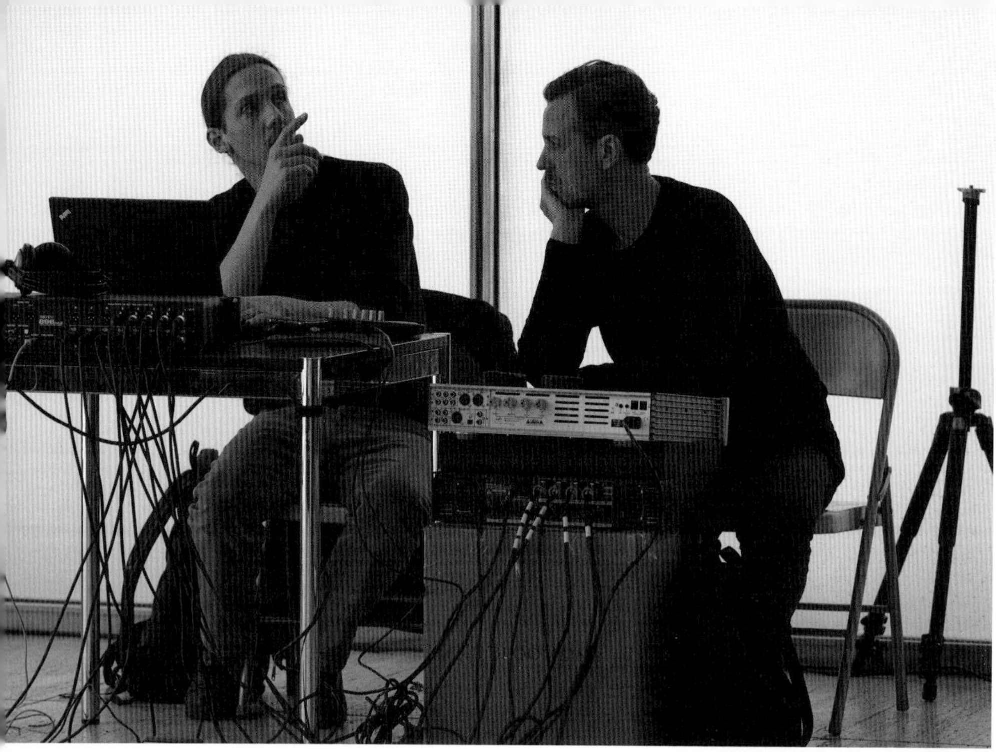

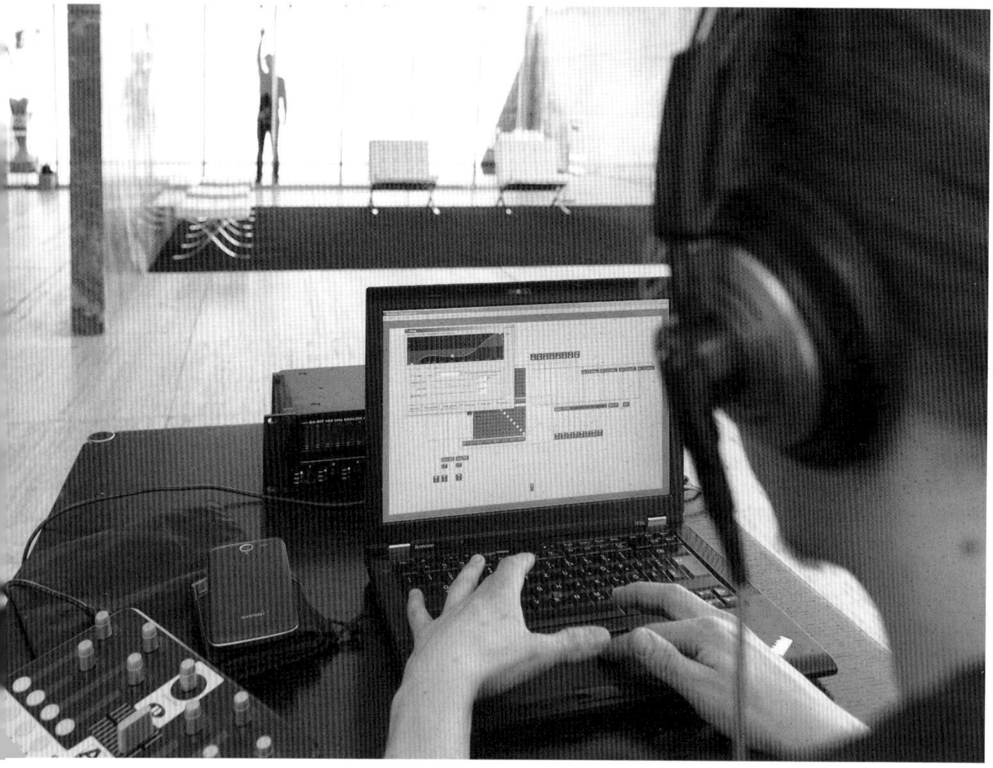

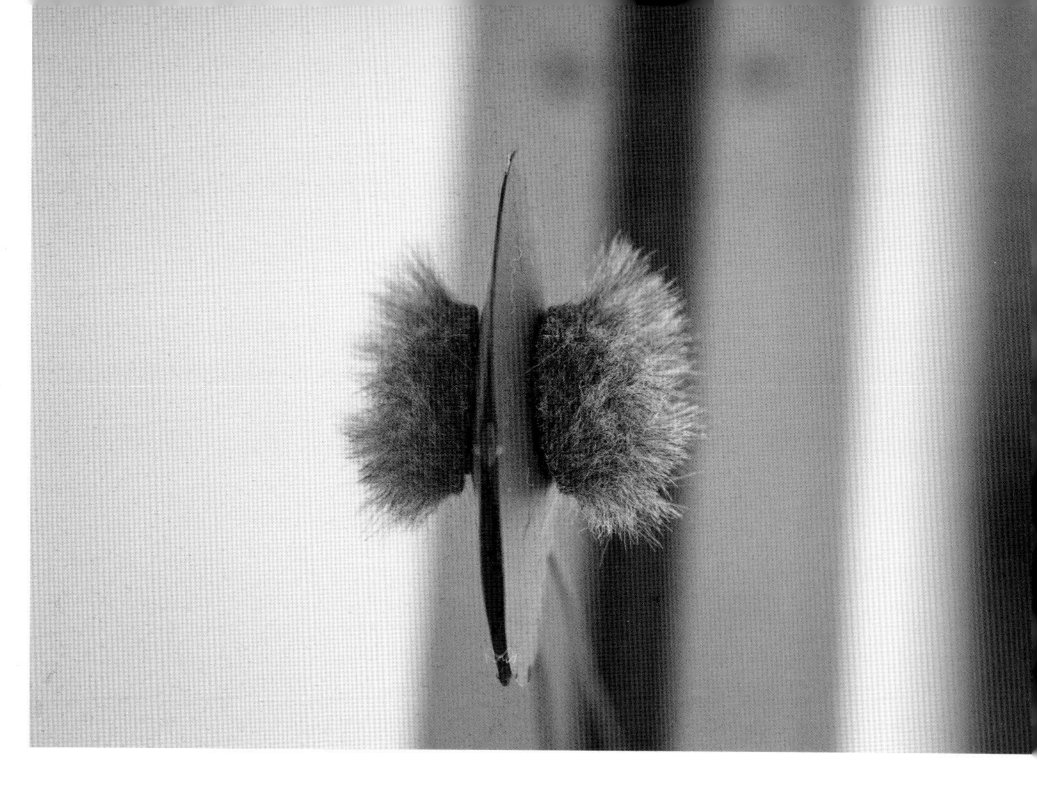

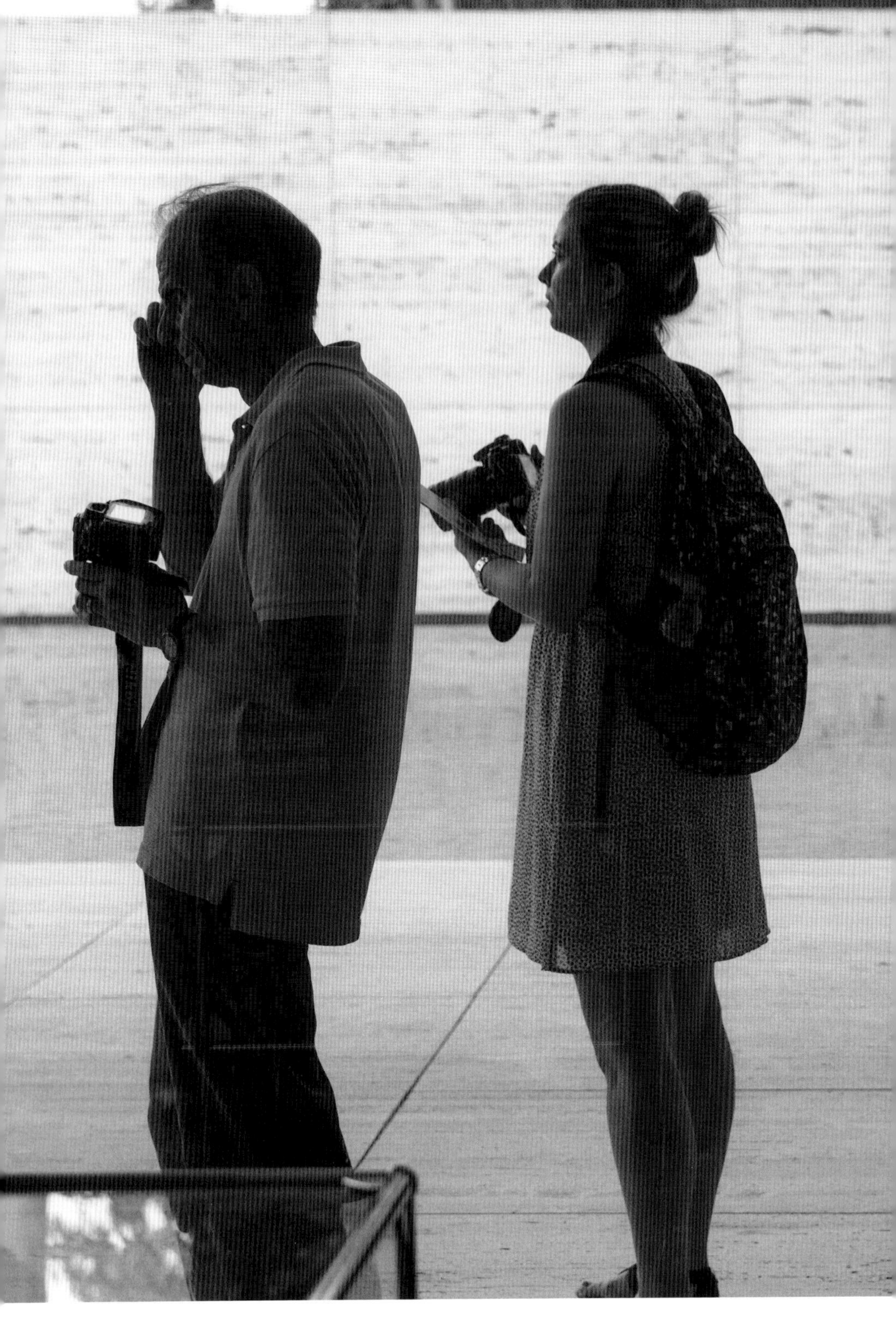

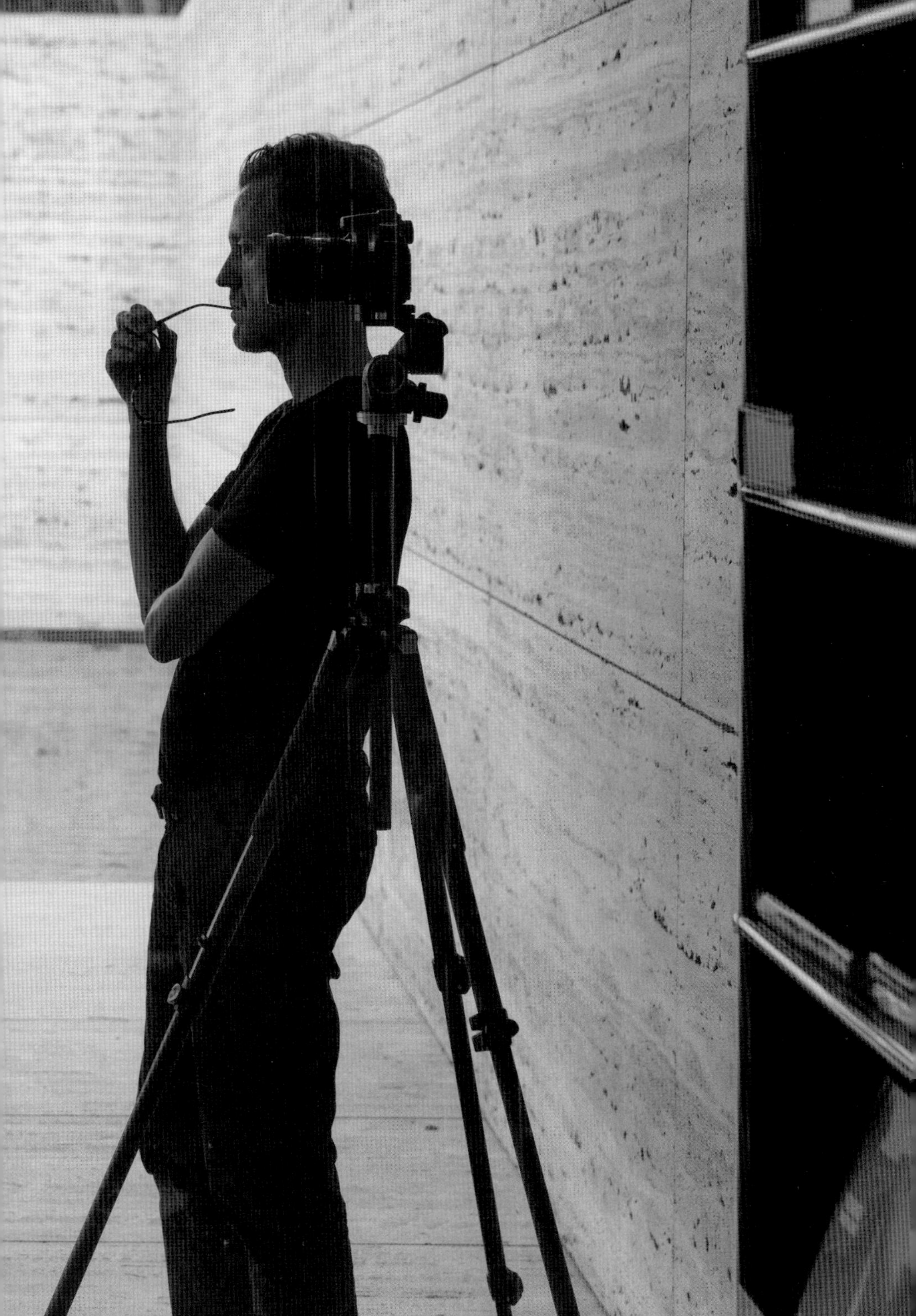

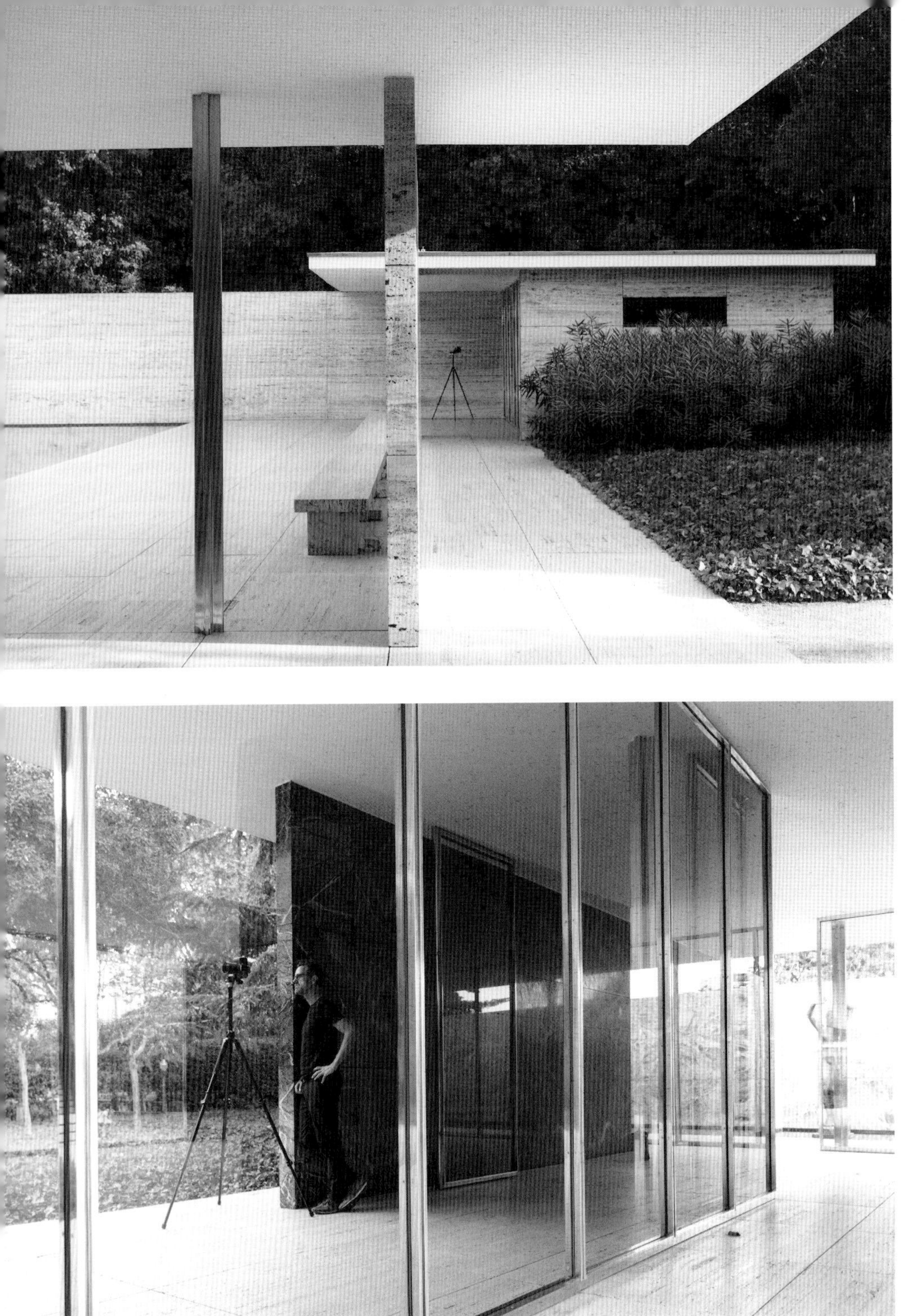

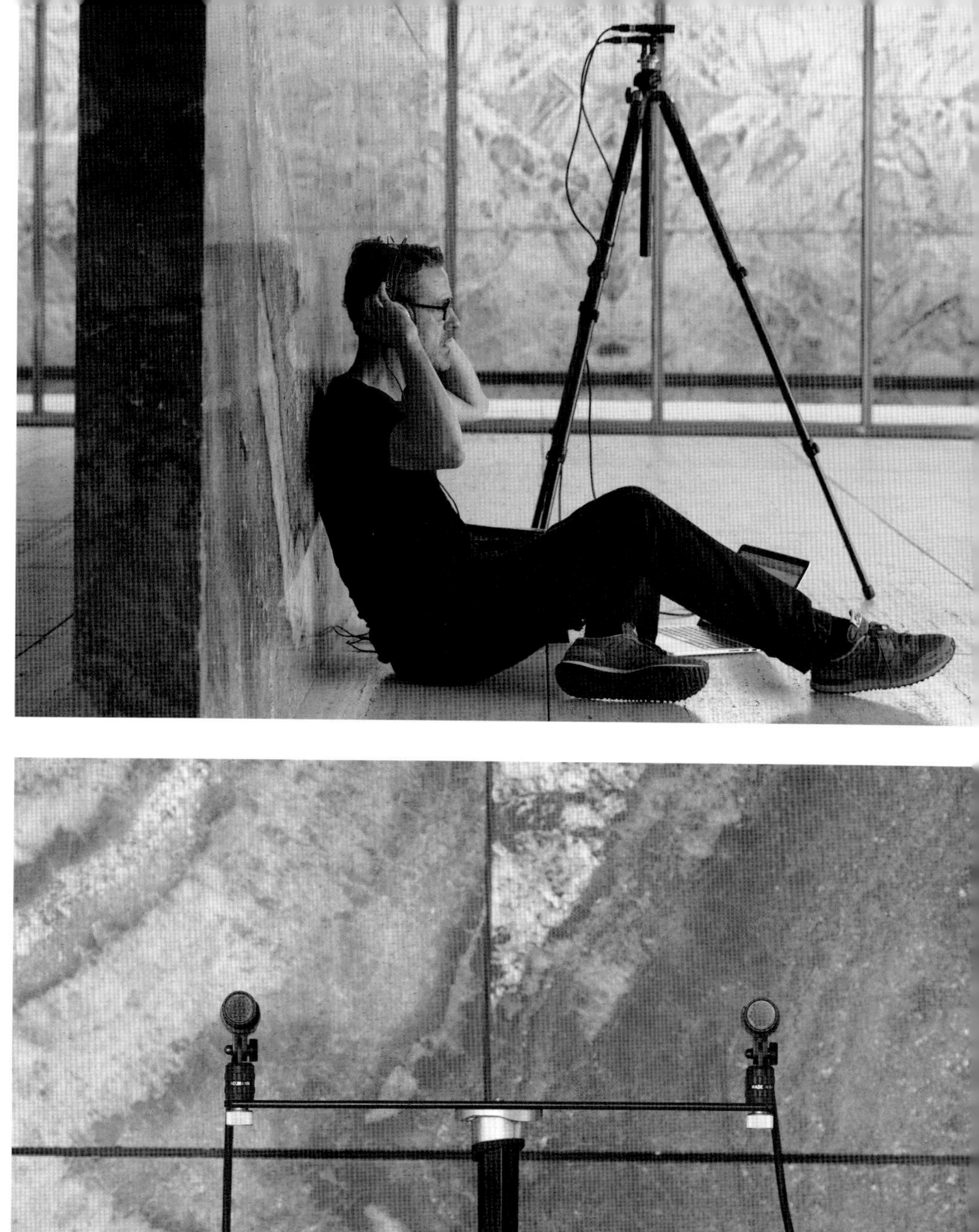

transient senses has been realized in the framework of Alex Arteaga's research project Architecture of Embodiment [www.architecture-embodiment.org], supported by the Einstein Foundation Berlin through an Einstein Junior Fellowship.

aknowledgements

I would like to express my gratitude to the Fundació Mies van der Rohe for giving me the opportunity to work in the Barcelona Pavilion. Especially to all its staff, who have provided the best possible conditions to develop this research and to produce this book. I also want to thank to the Fundació Banc de Sabadell their support for this project. I thank the Einstein Foundation Berlin for making the entire research project Architecture of Embodiment possible through an Einstein Junior Fellowship. I would like to warmly thank Lluís Nacenta for inviting me to realize this project, and for honoring the word "curator" with his attentive and careful support. My thanks also go to the Goethe-Institut Barcelona, very particularly and cordially to Ursula Wahl for trusting this endeavor from the beginning, and for moving other people and institutions to support it as well. I would like to recognize the contribution of the Fundació Antoni Tàpies, which offered the concentrated atmosphere of its spaces for the presentation of the essays. Recognition also goes to EINA, University School of Design and Art of Barcelona, and more concretely to the staff of the MURAD, an MA in art and design research, for co-organizing the research seminar. Further recognition goes to Sónar+D and especially Enric Palau, Jose Luis de Vicente, and Astrid Rousse for supporting the whole project in different ways. I thank the Institute Français of Barcelona as well for its aid in the realization of the seminar.

With respect to the realization of the sound installation, I would like to express my thanks to Thomas Koch for the technological implementation of my ideas and for the long conversations that helped me to better understand them. I also thank Daisuke Ishida for supporting the programming work. I am thankful to Leo de Klerk, not only for having invented the Omniwave loudspeakers, but especially for his thoughtful and expert advice regarding their specific use in this production. I would like to express my most sincere gratitude to Víctor Sánchez and part of his team—Ruth Castilla, Manuel Luque, Marc Quintana, and Alex Raya—for making the installation possible, and for engaging in this endeavor beyond the strict limits of their professional obligations. In the same sense I would like to kindly thank Linda Valdés for enabling the exhibition of the essays at the Fundació Antoni Tàpies. For his technical advice on the realization of the video essay, I would like to thank Björn Speidel.

I would like to express my gratitude as well to Michael Turnbull for his committed and sensitive work as editor of the text essays and for copy editing the whole volume, as well as to Sage Anderson for her dedicated copy editing of the other texts.. My very special thanks also go to the experts who participated in the research seminar: Susanne Hauser, Dieter Mersch, Gerard Vilar, Rudolf Bernet, Jean-Paul Thibaud, and Xavier Bassas. They exceptionally enriched the course of this research process. I want to thank Lucio Capece as well for his artistic contribution to the second part of the seminar.

For making transient senses and Architecture of Embodiment possible on the level of practical, everyday development, I would like to sincerely thank my assistant Lucas Hövelmann, as well as Mirko Behrens in representation of the Berlin Career College and the MA Sound Studies and Sonic Arts, both at the Berlin University of the Arts.

For the realization and publication of this book I would like to express my most cordial gratitude to the publisher RM, especially to Ramón Reverté and Lea Tyrallova. I would thank Thomas Vilhelm as well for his fine and attentive gaze, and for its materialization in the photographs included in this volume. In the same sense, I thank Adrià Sunyol and his team for the realization of the documentary of the research seminar.

And last but not least I want to express my most sincere gratitude and respect to Ricardo Duque and Tiago Pina from the design and communication studio todojunto for the design of this book.

They have all made possible what you now have in your hands.

transient senses, first edition 2016 — Texts: © Alex Arteaga. — Photographs: © Thomas Vilhelm.
Editorial and artistic consultant: Ramón Reverté. — Publication coordination: Lea Tyrallová.
Copy editing: Michael Turnbull, Sage Anderson — Design: todojunto.net. — Production coordination:
200bis — Printing: Agpograf. — Letterpress on covers: L'Automàtica — Print run: 1,000 copies.
Printed in Spain. #279 — ISBN: 978-84-16282-67-8. — Depósito Legal: B 19267-2016.
© 2016. RM Verlag, S.L. Loreto 13-15, local B, 08029, Barcelona, Spain.
© 2016. Editorial RM, S. A. de C. V. Río Pánuco 141, Col. Cuauhtémoc, 06500 Mexico D. F., Mexico.
info@editorialrm.com — www.editorialrm.com.
Fundació Mies van der Rohe — Director: Anna Ramos — Executive director: Antoni Garijo
Prize Coordinator: Ivan Blasi — Coordination: Anna Giró.